USE SOCIAL MEDIA TO FIND YOUR DREAM JOB!

How to Use LinkedIn, Google+, Facebook, Twitter and Other Social Media in Your Job Search

Dan Quillen & Dr. Lance Farr

Dan is the author of *The Perfect Resume, The Perfect Interview, Your First Job*, and *Get a Job! How I Found a Job When Jobs are Hard to Find – And So Can You!* Lance is a pioneer in the use of Social Media job searching.

Cold Spring Press
Get a Job! series

PRAISE FOR QUILLEN & FARR

"I was out of work for almost 2 years, and was just not getting many responses from the resumes I was sending out. I picked up a copy of Dan's book and began following his counsel in a number of areas, especially related to resumes and interviewing. Within 3 weeks, I had 4 interviews and received two job offers. I am now happily employed with a great job and feel like following Dan's counsel is the primary reason I was able to get these job offers and land my job." – *Jeremy Savage*

"Dan Quillen knows what he is talking about. I took his advice and had a job within 3 weeks of being laid off. Buy it today and it will set you on a direct course to success!" – *Lynette W. Fox*

"Mr. Quillen's *Get a Job!* is an easy read with a great deal of helpful information. Having been a hiring manager and HR director, as well as having been laid off himself during the recent recession, Mr. Quillen has a particular expertise that others may not. This book is also written with a focus on how techniques in job searching have changed in recent years, due to technology and the economy. I highly recommend this book to those that are either newly unemployed or wishing to make a change." – *Debra S. Heglin*

"I have been recommending *The Perfect Resume* to all my candidates. I love the content and the order of things that are presented in Dan's book." – *Sally S. Cohen, President, The Arundel Group*

"Lance is a powerful presenter and has a great teaching style. He is effective in presenting complex topics and taking advantage of social media to make his point. He has a great classroom personality. It is a pleasure to be in one of his classes." – *Tom Flodeen*

"Dr. Farr is an extremely knowledgeable and dynamic individual. He has expertise in the job search and networking market. I learned so much talking and working with him." – *Janet Ulrich, Services Architect*

USE SOCIAL MEDIA TO FIND YOUR DREAM JOB!

How to Use LinkedIn, Google+, Facebook, Twitter and Other Social Media in Your Job Search

Dan Quillen & Dr. Lance Farr

COLD SPRING PRESS
www.get-a-great-job.com

Copyright © 2016 by Dan Quillen & Lance Farr
ISBN 13: 978-1-59360-196-6
Library of Congress Control Number: 2016937083

See page 125 for information about the authors.

Table of Contents

USE SOCIAL MEDIA TO FIND YOUR DREAM JOB!

Introduction

Thank you for picking up *Use Social Media to Find Your Dream Job!* If you've purchased this book, or checked it out from the library, or it has been given to you by a friend or family member, it probably means you are out of work or working and looking for a change. Either way, you are looking for work, and you have correctly surmised that using all the tools in your job search toolbox – including social media – is key to your success in finding a job.

While the economy has shown some improvement recently and employers are cautiously optimistic, job seekers still face challenges in convincing those employers they are the answers to their employment problems.

Are you one of many of our nation's job seekers who is simply not having success? You have a sparkling resume that you tailor for each job for which you apply. You've brushed up on your interviewing skills and feel confident you can nail any interview to which you are invited. You've gotten the word out through your network that you are seeking work. And you still haven't found a job. If that's the case, you may want to spend a few hours perusing the pages of this book.

You'll learn about how to make the most efficient use of social media as you search for your job. Used properly, **social media can help you discover jobs** that aren't available elsewhere, can help you communicate with your network that you are seeking employment, and get your name and brand in front of recruiters and hiring managers.

In today's job-search landscape, you have to be a savvy seeker. You have to be qualified. You have to be persistent. You have to know how to present yourself and overcome obstacles that crop up to mar your employment search. And you need to use all the tools that are available to you in order to successfully end your unemployment / under-employment. Social media can do just that, and that's what this book is all about.

Naturally, you may have a few questions about this book. There are a number of books about using social media to find work on the market – what makes this one different? Why should you purchase it, or listen to what it has to say? Let's see if we can answer those and other questions you may have:

What qualifies these guys to write this book?
For the past six years, on a daily basis, Lance has worked closely with a multitude of job seekers, helping them create their own personal brand through social media and use that most effective tool to get their name in front of recruiters and hiring managers. Many have benefited from his guidance and advice on how best to use social media to maximize their job search. And – many have been successful in their job searches and ended their unemployment.

Dan has been a Human Resource professional for nearly twenty-five years, and for longer than that, he has been a hiring manager. He knows what hiring managers and HR departments look for when screening applicants and resumes for positions. And – perhaps more important – he knows what works and what does not work for applicants when it comes to job searches. As a bonus, he used social media in his own job hunt to help bring his personal job search to a successful end.

You may know Dan from several of the other job-search books he has written: *Get a Job!, The Perfect Resume, The Perfect Interview* and *Your First Job: The Recent Grad's Indispensable Guide to Getting a Job.*

Why are these guys writing this book?
So many job seekers today don't realize the incredible advantage using social media will give them to bring their job search to a successful conclusion. Most in today's society are aware of social media – Facebook, Twitter, LinkedIn and Google+ -- but many haven't used those tools to advance their job search.

Both Lance and Dan have made careers out of helping people find work – it's what they do. They enjoy sharing their expertise in various areas of successful job searches, and enjoy helping people break though the barriers to re-employment. Now, instead of working one-on-one with these job seekers, they are using this book to reach many more and (hopefully) help many others find work in this improving-yet-still-difficult economy.

These guys know what they're talking about – I should listen to them!

Our hope is that through the pages of this book you can learn a few key principles about using social media to bring your job search to a successful – and profitable – conclusion.

We are interested in hearing how things are going in your job search, especially as you use the concepts relating to social media that we cover in this book. When you have a chance, please e-mail us at *SocialMedia4DreamJob@gmail.com* and let us know how it is going, your successes and even some of your questions. Especially let us know if you are successful in your job search by using some of the techniques we present in this book. Who knows? Your experience might be highlighted in a future edition!

Overview

Thank you for your interest in *Use Social Media to Find Your Dream Job!* Over the next hundred-plus pages, we'll spend a little time together, discussing information you should know about using powerful social media tools in your job search. The job search landscape has changed in recent years, and using social media in your job search will help you beat the competition to that job you are so earnestly seeking.

The economy today is improving over what it has been for the last few years…but it's still a tough market in which to find work. Without social media, you're handicapping yourself in your job search.

Following is what we'll show you in this book about using social media:

In **Chapter 1**, *Introduction*, we'll talk about the importance of using social media in your job search, and we outline our credentials that allow us to write this book – in particular our efforts over the past few years that were targeted toward those who were in the same situation as you – out of work and seeking that next opportunity.

In **Chapter 3**, *Your Situation*, you'll learn that there is "The Job" – the job you will want to get out of bed to go to. But – you'll also learn that you may need to change the way you conduct your job search in order to find "The Job" because the pain of continuing to search the way you have been searching is greater than the pain of changing and learning new things.

In **Chapter 4**, *Goals and Objectives*, you'll learn the simple premise that your Number One goal should be to get The Job. The number of resumes you submit, the number of interviews you're invited to, mean nothing if you don't get the job.

In **Chapter 5**, *Aim at Their Pain*, we'll spend a few pages discussing how to determine what pain your potential employer is experiencing, and how you show them you are the antidote to their pain!

In **Chapter 6**, *LinkedIn, The Job Market*, we'll walk you through the process to complete a critical social media tool for your job search – a professional LinkedIn profile. Make sure you include a professional photograph with your profile!

In **Chapter 7**, *LinkedIn, The Search Engine*, you'll learn how to make connections and then use them to help get you to the hiring manager. And – it's not just good for you – it can be good for them as well.

In **Chapter 8**, *Facebook*, you'll learn that Facebook is more than a place to read political rants and see dancing cats. It's a viable – although potentially dangerous – place to conduct your job search. Learn what is meant by Puritan clean.

In **Chapter 9**, *Stay Positive!*, we take a break from reviewing social media options and explore the need for you to stay positive during your job search. Negativity can creep into cover letters, interviews, even resumes – and you must guard against this! Negativity is not a sought-after characteristic by employers and recruiters.

In **Chapter 10**, *Twitter and G+*, you'll learn how to use these two great social media tools to find jobs, make contacts and follow people who may be beneficial to your job search.

In **Chapter 11**, *Showcase Your Expertise*, you'll learn about these online options to providing yet another way for people to learn more about you, your skills and experience.

In **Chapter 12**, *E-mail*, addresses the homeliest of social media tools – e-mail. While not as svelte and sexy as some of the other social media giants, it is still a valuable tool that can and should be used in your job search.

In **Chapter 13**, *Getting Company Information*, you'll learn the value of Reference USA – a website that was seemingly designed to provide much-needed company information to job seekers. You'll also learn how to master the skill of Google-fu – a great job search application that many job seekers are unaware of.

In **Chapter 14**, *Homework*, we'll take you through a few steps to help you learn an unbelievable amount of information about the companies for which you may be interested in working.

In **Chapter 15**, *Resumes*, you'll learn that even though this is a book on social media, you still need to have a top-notch, tailored resume to be successful in getting an interview.

In **Chapter 16**, *Common Resume Errors*, we'll talk about some of the most common errors we see in resumes. Read this chapter carefully so you don't commit any of these all-too-common mistakes.

In **Chapter 17**, *In Closing*, we spend a few minutes highlighting some of the key points we made throughout the book to refresh your memory and to help get you excited about going out and trying some of these techniques yourself.

So let's go – strap on your job-search seatbelt, and let's figure out how you can make this chapter in your life as short as possible!

Your Situation

"It was the best of times, it was the worst of times…" At least that is what Charles Dickens said in his 1859 novel, *A Tale of Two Cities*. We could certainly say the same about finding a job today! There are more jobs available at the beginning of 2016 than there have been in the past six to eight years. The unemployment rate has dramatically dropped from double digits and has been reported to be near 3% in many areas of the country.

Yet it seems as difficult as it has ever been to find a job. Especially "The Job" you want. You know, "That Job" – the job you look forward to getting out of bed to go to. It just doesn't seem right does it? You are either suffering with a miserable position or two, barely able to keep the bill collectors away or not working at all. The frustration and discouragement can be daunting.

But…what if you knew how to **BE FOUND** by the recruiter who has "The Job" – "That Job" – and is trying desperately to find you? What is that worth to you? What are you willing to do? Are you willing to change how you go about your job search? Are you willing to admit you may be going about things the wrong way, that there could be a better way today than there was yesterday? Do you understand what Tony Robbins meant when he said:

> *Change happens when the pain of staying the same is greater than the pain of change.*

If so, welcome my friend. Experience has taught us we likely have something of great value for you. If you don't find yourself in that position, be brave, go into waters in which you have not

What is the pain I am experiencing by staying in the situation I am now in?

ventured. Knowledge is power. Power to change, power to influence, power to grow. Besides, you already purchased the book. What have you got to lose (other than your unemployment check!)?

Recruiter's point of view

In today's recruiting world, it often takes more than simply sending in resumes and filling out applications to get hired. Most recruiters burned out on that long ago. Since at least 2008, with real unemployment soaring into double digits and millions of Americans receiving unemployment, recruiters were buried by applicants who were required to complete five job applications each week to continue to receive their much-needed unemployment benefits. Whether the applicant was qualified for the job or would relocate for it was simply never considered. The result was an onslaught of more than 200 job applications and resumes for every posted job!

This fundamentally changed the way recruiters and HR departments searched for viable candidates to interview and hire. For these folks the pain of doing the same thing was greater than the pain of change! What changes did they make? How can you leverage those changes? Well, that is what you are about to learn!

Your Situation checklist

_____ The economy is improving, but I am still seeking employment.

_____ I may need to change the way I have been conducting my job search.

_____ Has my pain increased to the point where I am willing to change the way I have been conducting my job search?

_____ "That Job" – the job I can't wait to get out of bed to go to – is waiting for me to find it!

_____ Recruiters have changed the way they seek for candidates – I need to make myself easy for them to find me.

4 Goals and Objectives

Get "The Job"
Your only real goal and objective is to get "The Job." Never – and we mean never – forget that. It is not about how many resumes you sent, or how many interviews you got (or didn't get), who you know or don't know. **It is all about Getting The Job**. Period. But like all real goals there is a plan of milestones to meet. A successful business is more than an idea. It is a detailed, fluid plan built on experience and knowledge. That experience and knowledge teaches what must be firmly entrenched and what must be flexible. Please pay attention to these. It is very important to your successful job hunt.

Enough small talk. Let's look at the outline of what we will be doing:

Goals and Objectives
   1. Become known by your industry peers and hiring managers.

   2. Establish yourself as an expert in your field.

   3. Ensure potential employers and recruiters can find you easily.

      a. Finding a job to apply for is easy, being found by a recruiter is where it's at!

Prescription for finding a job
1. Find a company you want to work for (Use Reference USA, company social media pages, reputation, networking contacts, etc.

> "The employer has a pain and you are the relief."
> – Dr. Lance Farr

17

2. Find a job posting for which you are qualified.

3. Make yourself look like the job posting on your social media sites and resume.

4. Find a networking contact to deliver your social media profile and resume to the decision maker for that job.

Advantages of using social media
A few advantages come to mind:

1. It demonstrates you are current in today's cyber age. (Especially important for the over-40 job seeker.)

2. You get to build *interactive* relationships with key industry players.

3. You learn **what and who** the employer is looking for and an immediate way for you to get in front of the employer.

Social media tools we will explore
1. LinkedIn

2. Facebook

3. Twitter

4. Others social media such as: Blogs, Reference USA, YouTube, E-mail, Personal Websites

LinkedIn
1. We'll show you how to build your profile so recruiters will find you and demonstrate your industry expertise (studies show that having a professional-looking picture on your LinkedIn profile makes it *fourteen times more likely to be found!*).

2. There are over 400 million users and millions of jobs and employers on LinkedIn.

3. 94% of recruiters use LinkedIn to find and analyze candidates, while only 36 % of job seekers are active on LinkedIn (Jobvite 2014).

4. Network three levels deep (you'll learn more about this later).

5. Automatic mapping of network to companies and jobs.

6. There are in excess of three million jobs on LinkedIn with 44,000 being added every second.

7. Group discussions are available to you which will enable you to establish yourself as an expert in the field.

8. **Be found by employers** who are searching for an employee with your skills and experience!

Blog (YouTube, Shutterfly, etc.)
    1. Demonstrates and showcases:
        a. Your current expertise and industry involvement.

        b. Showcases your relevant achievements, skills, projects and ideas.

        c. Easily shared with important industry contacts.

        d. Demonstrates your value to potential employers.

Twitter
    1. Find, connect with and follow hiring managers.

    2. Identify job postings.

    3. Be followed by your industry leaders.

    4. Notify the "the world" you are an expert in your field.
        a. And that you're looking for a new opportunity.

    5. Company official web page.

Facebook
     1. Network of ready and willing contacts.

     2. Company pages
          a. Learn what is important to companies in which you are interested – what their current initiatives are and what community causes are they are involved in.

          b. Who is actively involved from the company (source of networking contacts).

          c. Current job postings.

     3. Employers will use it to check you out by looking at your profile and who your friends are.
          a. and what you and your friends and family members have to say about controversial topics of the day.

Oiling the Social Media Machine
     1. Get Hired!

     2. The Goal: be found and approached by the employer.

     3. Understand the employers' needs.

     4. *Aim at their pain!*

Okay – so why does all this matter? What's in it for you? We want to give you a teaser here. Within just a few pages, we are going to teach you some principles that apply directly to successful job searches. Before trying them in job searches, Lance tried them on a hobby of his: teaching scuba. He figured if he could make this work for one of his hobbies (one that does not exactly change the world!) it could work for a job seeker as well. So he did it, and did it work?

You be the judge: After he finished his plan, if you were to have searched Google for the term "scuba," you would have found Lance was the number eight hit out of millions of hits! His name came up before the scuba resorts, manufacturers, dive shops, etc. – in other words, the entire scuba industry. All of them were following Lance worldwide, from the big play-ers right on down to individual divers. It was simple and fun to do and the best part was it only took Lance a few weeks to do it. If he wanted a career in the scuba industry, he had all the contacts he could have ever hoped for and was seen as an industry expert by them. More on this story later, when it will make more sense.

This is the kind of exposure we have been able to gain for our job seekers as we have worked with them in their job searches. And as often as not, we were able to cut their unemployment time in half from what other job seekers who weren't using social media were experiencing.

Goals and Objectives checklist

_____ Resumes submitted, interviews invited to, etc., don't matter unless I get The Job. That should be my Number One goal.

_____ I need to make myself known to recruiters and hiring managers.

_____ I need to establish myself as an expert in my field.

_____ I need to be the antidote to the pain my future employer is feeling.

_____ LinkedIn, blogs, Facebook, Twitter, Google+ are all tools that will help me accomplish my objective – get "The Job!"

_____ I need to understand my employer's needs.

Aim at Their Pain

All employers who are in the recruiting market are experiencing pain. They need a skilled, educated and experienced employee to bring value to their organization. The three questions that you must ask are:

1. What skill?

2. How much education?

3. What experiences do they require?

It is *sooooo* easy to find the answers to their questions, yet nearly all job seekers miss the mark. The employer tells you specifically what they want in the job posting! *That* is their pain.

So let us first look at how to address these employer pain points in a manner that is meaningful to the employer. *Please understand it is what the employer wants to see that is important, not what you want to show them.*

Let us repeat that again:

Please understand it is what the employer wants to see that is important, not what you want to show them.

You can have all the social media sites and contacts you want, but if you do not show how your value satisfies the employer's needs, who cares? Certainly not the employer!

Everything we do is going to be based on what we call an **Achievement Statement**. The formula is a simple one: **S**ituation, **A**ction, **R**esult, or **SAR**. But what we always want to tell our audience is the *result*. Responsibilities and actions *without results* are not very impressive. For all the reader or listener knows you may have been one of the worst employees ever to do that particular job. You want to show them that you were better than the average run-of-the-mill employee – you need to show your value.

So let's say you're a sales manager looking for your next opportunity, and you discover a job posting for a *Senior Sales Manager, Software*.

You might be tempted to write something like:

> Responsibilities and actions without results are not very impressive!

> I was a national sales manager for fifteen years. I was known for being hardworking, loyal and I was the go-to guy for a variety of situations.

Sounds pretty good, doesn't it? But what does it really tell us? "Sales Manager." I suppose that means this person managed sales, or did he/she manage a sales force, or maybe organized the sales numbers and reports? OK… "National" ummm? Does this mean this sales manager had one sales person who worked in the four-corners area and sold kettle corn in "all four states" at the local gift shops? "Loyal, hardworking and go-to guy." That sounds more like my bird dog than a valuable employee. Those qualities along with integrity are absolute requirements for *all* jobs. I have yet to see a job posting requiring any of these characteristics (loyalty and hardworking). Nor does the above statement give your audience – the hiring manager or recruiter –- any sort of feeling of accomplishment, success or value above and beyond the required minimum.

Let's see what can be done to show what we really did, and what value we brought to the company. Think about the following: Can we quantify? Demonstrate success? Give scope or breadth? What if you said:

> I was a Sales Manager for Oracle for fifteen years covering ten western states. I managed 150 of the brightest sales professionals in the industry. By creating an analytical data base, actively

listening to our customer needs and understanding the strengths and weaknesses of our many viable competitors I trained and led this talented team to the top. Together we met or exceeded every annual sales goal with an approximate average of 104% of our target. We were awarded the "Golden Hammer" by the CEO four times for being the top-producing sales team in the company.

Believe it or not, the two statements describe the same person! Who do you think the recruiter wants to talk with and who do you think the hiring manager offers the job to? Your job!

Achievement statements can be very powerful and even more effective when they are crafted to be short and to the point…really. We can be flexible here. Especially on resumes and profiles. A well-written achievement statement begs the reader to ask the question: "How did he/she do that?" When you can create that question in your potential employer's (or recruiter's) mind, you are head and shoulders above the competition.

Let's look at and example from an Industrial Engineer's resume:

> Redesigned manufacturing shop floor using CAD and Lean Six Sigma resulting in a 47% increase of productivity and a 25% decrease in work-related accidents.

"WOW. How did he/she do that? That is EXACTLY what we need done!" exclaims the recruiter as she/he hurriedly rushes to find the hiring manager! In other words – you have a job interview coming your way FAST!

Key Concept
As impressive as those achievement statements are, if the employer didn't have a manufacturing floor that needed redesigning, or if the recruiter wasn't scouting for a high-level sales manager, those stellar achievement statements are interesting, but miss the mark completely.

Here are six questions you can ask yourself to help you write out your achievements in a manner that is meaningful to your next employer:

1. What did I do for the company? (Not just my job title, but *what did I do?*)

2. Did I do it well?

3. How do I know I did it well, and how can I share that?

4. What value did I add to the company?

5. What did my boss write in my reviews?

6. How was my performance measured by the company?

Get it? Most of us have a tendency to speak in responsibilities and activities, not achievements. The employer already knows your basic responsibilities, which is why he is looking at your profile! Nobody says, "I need a national sales manager, I'm going to look at industrial engineers." **Your achievements** are what will show your expertise, your ability to work and play well with others and make you stand out from the crowd.

Sometimes it is difficult to talk about ourselves in this manner, especially if you were raised by a mother like mine, who taught us not to brag about ourselves! But did our moms brag about our children! In a word – Yes! It is important here to note, you are not bragging. You are merely demonstrating to the employer you have what they are looking for, that you offer the much-needed pain relief they are seeking.

Excerpts from your past reviews can be a wonderful source of material for achievement statements. Your reviews are justification from your boss to his or her boss showing your contributions, why you should keep your job, get a raise and maybe even a promotion.

Dan's resume has the following excerpt from one of his performance reviews when he was director of Human Resources at a large law firm:

> *Dan communicates very well; he knows when to talk and write like an employment lawyer, and when to talk and write like a Director of Human Resources. (Written comment in performance review by an employment law partner with whom I worked extensively.)*

That comment garnered more comments and questions from hiring managers than just about any other items on Dan's resume. And it positioned him well with the hiring managers he met with.

Other effective sources of information about you are letters of reference from former supervisors. So – if you're calling them to get copies of your previous performance evaluations, consider asking them to provide you with a letter of reference.

Better yet – write the letter for them and ask them to edit the letter so that they are satisfied with it. Dan had a somewhat relcutant boss, so he offered to write it for him. Fortunately, Dan had kept his previous performance reviews from when he worked for him, so he went and cherry-picked those positive comments that related to the jobs he was applying for. Dan's boss was comfortable with the words he had once written and gladly signed what Dan wrote for him. Here it is, all taken from previous performance reviews he had given Dan over the course of seven years:

Dear Hiring Manager:

In the legal services industry, conventional wisdom is that when you are filling a critical and sensitive role such as Director of Human Resources, the candidate you select should have relevant law firm experience. When Dan Quillen interviewed for that role at Holme Roberts & Owen, I saw in Dan qualities and attributes I felt would make him an excellent Director of Human Resources for our firm, despite his lack of direct experience with law firms.

Dan worked hard to learn the nuances and differences of the legal services industry and to adapt his professional background and experience to the law firm culture. He acknowledged key stakeholders and worked well with individuals at all levels of the firm.

Dan proved to be an excellent Director of Human Resources for our firm. He demonstrated calm and professional judgment in fulfilling his responsibilities. Human relations and all that revolves around those elements of his role can be sensitive and volatile at times, and included in Dan's strengths are his demeanor and approach to such instances.

In addition to his skills in employee relations, Dan worked at becoming an expert in our benefits plans. This was not an area of focus for him with previous employers. His efforts in this regard allowed him to negotiate successfully with our carriers, resulting in significant savings for our firm. Over one three-year period, these savings surpassed $1,000,000.

One of Dan's main responsibilities was to help protect the firm from lawsuits for employment-related issues. During his ten years with the firm, Dan was responsible for the termination of over 200 individuals. Yet, despite the fact that individuals in law firms can often be more litigious by nature than the rest of the population, not one lawsuit was filed against the firm for employment-related actions. This was of inestimable value to the firm. One of the employment law partners with whom Dan worked closely observed in her written performance review for him: *"Dan communicates very well; he knows when to talk and write like an employment lawyer, and when to talk and write like an HR Director."*

Because Dan's skill set extended beyond human resources, we were able to ask him to fill the role of Director of Legal Recruiting on an interim basis when that Director left the firm. While continuing with his HR Director role, Dan was able to step up and fulfill the responsibilities associated with this additional role for 18 months until we could find a suitable candidate to fill this role. Dan's efforts in this regard saved the firm over $200,000 during this period.

Dan enjoyed the respect of lawyers, staff and his colleagues on the senior management team. I can recommend him for any senior HR positions you may have for which he has the skills and experience you are seeking. If you have any questions, please contact me at 314-555-1212.

Very truly yours,

He then signed the letter over his title (Chief Operating Officer). The letter was written on his firm's letterhead.

Once you have your letters of reference, create PDFs of the documents. The next time an interviewer asks the all-too-common question, "What would your former employer say about you?" You respond with a verbal answer of achievements, then reach into your portfolio and produce a copy of the letter! (That is not really social media, it is just a free hint on interviewing. After all, we want you to do well when you get to your interview!)

My achievement statements must match the employer's needs!

Now please take a break and go write out answers to the six questions at the top of page 25. The next section will be more meaningful if you do.

Pain Relief

Now that you have articulated, in a written format, some of the value you brought to former employers, we have a sure foundation to work on. Here comes one of the fun parts: Aiming at their pain!!!! Talk about putting yourself in the driver's seat! This is where you strap yourself in and light the fuse!

Go to Google or Monster.com or Indeed.com and find a job for which you are qualified and for which you would like to apply.

OK, good. Now, for *each* required qualification, that is each pain point, write an achievement statement. Try to keep it to less than three lines. You may find at first they come out rather long. That is to be expected. Look at what you wrote in detail. Is there really more than one achievement in the statement? Most likely.

Let's look at my Sales Manager example:

> "I was the Sales Manager for Oracle for fifteen years covering the ten western states. I managed 150 of the brightest sales professionals in the industry. By creating an analytical data base, actively listening to our customer needs and understand-

ing the strengths and weakness of our many viable competitors I trained and led this talented team to the top. Together we met or exceeded every annual sales goal with an approximate average of 104% of our target. We were awarded the annual "Golden Hammer" by the CEO four times for being the top producing sales team in the company, only awarded to one team per year."

Now take your pencil (if you actually own one! Lance had to take one from his 5th grader) and underline each separate concept which should be its own statement. … Go ahead and do it…. How many did you come up with? We came up with five:

Situation
I was the Sales Manager for Oracle for fifteen years covering the ten western states. I managed 150 of the brightest sales professionals in the industry.

Achievements
1. By creating an analytical data base,

2. actively listening to our customer needs and

3. understanding the strengths and weakness of our many viable competitors

4. I trained and led this talented team to the top

5. Together we met or exceeded every annual sales goal with an approximate average of *(Result) 104% of our target.*

Special Recognition
We were awarded the annual "Golden Hammer" by the CEO four times for being the top producing sales team in the company, only awarded to one team per year."

Each one of these five achievements can be turned into its own short and powerful statement.

Get it? OK, good. Now go back and break them out. Each one. When you are done come back for the next step…it is an easy one. Important but easy.

Now you have a good feeling for what your next employer needs and how you can fulfill them. Go find four to six more job postings and see how well your achievement statements address the pain points of those employers. Be sure you are using the same industry key word and phrases the employer is. You may need to word-smith some or even write a few new ones. By the time you write these, there will not likely be too many more you will have to write. As a general rule of thumb, if you can write a good achievement statement for about 80% of the job requirements of the employer, as listed on the job posting, you are on the right track -- you have the skills and experiences necessary to apply for the position.

Take a break, get them done and come back to Chapter 6. We'll meet you there.

Aim at Their Pain checklist

_____ I must show my value to the hiring manager.

_____ I need succinct and quantifiable achievement statements.

_____ I can use excerpts from previous performance evaluations to show my potential employers how valuable I can be for them.

_____ Answer the six questions Lance and Dan pose about my previous employment.

_____ Employers are sharing their pains – their needs – in the job ads they post. What skills and experience do I have that meets those needs?

_____ Get letters of recommendation from my previous bosses.

6 LinkedIn – *The* Job Market

In this chapter we will learn how to write **an effective LinkedIn profile**. One which will be the foundation for your discovery by recruiters.

At the time of this writing we found 18,295 jobs on LinkedIn with the title Administrative Assistant, 129,071 jobs with the title Engineer, 651 jobs with the title CFO and 508 for CEO. We also found 577 people with the title Administrative Assistant (do you think they might know some key players in the companies you'd like to work for? Uhhh, yes!), 1,591 engineers, 88 CFOs and 588 CEOs. But here is the gold mine: 647 recruiters and 2,738 HR professionals. And these are just the ones showing their titles.

The recruiting company CyberCoders has 15,879 jobs on LinkedIn at the same moment. The 2014 JobVite report estimates 94% of recruiters use LinkedIn to find and vet candidates for positions! Yet only 36% of active job seekers were on LinkedIn. That is an inefficiency we can definitely take advantage of. So let's go get found!

Your LinkedIn Profile

Your LinkedIn profile is the main element recruiters and HR personnel will be looking at to judge if they want to interview you. It has greatly supplanted the resume. We guess you could say, it is the resume of the day! But you still need a resume – more on that in a later chapter.

Starting your LinkedIn profile is as easy as going to LinkedIn.com and filling in the blanks. So if you don't already have one go do it....we'll wait. Oh, one word to the wise: your e-mail address. Don't be silly or inappropriate. DingleballsChevyChort@lowrider.com probably does not help you get a job a Ford Motor Company, but it may at *Low Rider* magazine. Dan saw one he could not believe: SleepingWithTheBoss@... Um, how do we say "NO, NO, NO!" Try to use one with your name or industry...like say DrFarr@... or DanQHR@... or JeanPetroleumEngineer@... This will be one of the first items which will be seen. What message are you sending? Just make it simple and appropriate.

Hint: E-mails are not case sensitive. So feel free to use some upper case letters to make it readable and easy to remember. For example, Lance uses DrFarr@...

OK, if you're not already on LinkedIn, go sign up and come back. We need a short break here.

You should have the ability now to log into LinkedIn. Let's start building a profile with meaning, one which will get you found and an interview offered.

Name
Use your real name as it will appear on your resume and applications. It would be very unfortunate if in the hustle and bustle of the hiring process, a key player did not make the connection to Richard L. Farr and Lance Farr, or William D. Quillen and Dan Quillen. Both of us go by our middle name.

Experience
Current Job Title: Do not fudge here. If your title was "Team Lead" but your job looked more like a project manager, DON'T use Project Manager! A simple call to your former employer will reveal your correct job title and *voila!* You blew it! It looks like you tried to pull a fast one. I'll show you later how to communicate that you were really more of a PM than a team lead. Integrity is an expectation, as it should be.

Use the achievement statements you wrote based on the six current job postings you looked at. Be sure to use the same key words and phrases in your statements as are contained in the job postings. These key words are the same words that the recruiters will be using in their LinkedIn search. Remember also, recruiters are very rarely, if ever, subject matter experts in the industry. They are Human Resource and recruiting experts. With that in mind you will understand these Human Resource people and recruiters will be using word recognition when first reviewing your LinkedIn profile (and resume for that matter). So keep it simple for them.

For example, if you wrote: "Expert at writing programming language to integrate systems faster with higher efficiency." Our HR and recruiting experts may not recognize you just said you are an expert in Python programming language.

But if you had written: "Expert in Python programming, integrated six different systems with 3,500 end users nine days prior to the deadline and 3% under budget," you would have hit the mark. (By the way – that is a good achievement statement.)

HR and recruiters now see you have the Python programming language they are looking for (word recognition) and that you are likely good at it ("nine days prior to deadline and 3% under budget" – that is a very important and valuable part: the 'result.' It demonstrates your success) and you are budget conscious as well. So you would have not only helped our first-look people (HR and recruiting) see via word recognition you have the required Python programming skill, you also would have been able to add value: you're "Budget conscious" and meet deadlines. Always remember to quantify your results whenever possible.

Any hiring manager who will see these statements will instantly understand the great implications of what went into the entire process. They will also appreciate your time efficiency and budget control. Do you see how we are speaking to your entire audience?

Talk about relieving their pain points! How could they resist wanting to talk to you with a LinkedIn profile like this? Heck, we might even want to talk to you and we don't even know what we'd do with a Python expert!

Don't be afraid to use awards and accolades as well. Here are a couple of examples: "Praised in team meeting for intuitive thinking." Or "Won the 'Golden Hammer' award for most 'cold calls' in the year. Only given to one sales professional each year." Notice, we qualified the unknown. That is, if only one award is given each year, it has much more value than "given to the top 10% each quarter."

Try to stay away from clichés like: "Go-to person." Honestly, that has more use than an L.A. freeway. Instead, try something like: "Often used as a team resource for problem solving. For example: reviewing and correcting programming errors prior to beta testing, resulting in shorter testing periods and getting the product to the customer faster." Isn't that much better than "go-to person" – it is certainly more specific and descriptive. Here is another one: "Excellent written and verbal communication skills." We wish we had a dime for every time we read that one! If you take the time and effort to make your LinkedIn, Facebook and other profiles as well as your cover letters and resumes look and read the way you are being taught here, you will have demonstrated excellent written skills. If you interview in a good conversational manner using these same techniques, you will have validated your verbal skills as well. But no matter what, as soon as you start to speak, that judgment will begin to form the interviewer's opinion…another free tip!

The same applies to all your former positions. Go get those done and then we will go on the next area.

I must hone my LinkedIn profile to perfection!

Education

Use your highest level of education, include your GPA if it is worth bragging about, like say a 3.75 on a 4.0 scale or better. You can also put your Latin designation of honor. For example, show *Magna Cum Laude*, but not *Cum Laude*. For sure if you were *Summa Cum Laude*! There are companies and management programs which will require a minimum GPA – they will ask for it on the application, so you will have to include it even if it isn't 3.75+.

Photograph

A professional photograph will increase the likelihood of your LinkedIn profile being looked at by 14%! Do it! By a "professional" photograph, that means one in a business suit with a non-distracting background. It does not mean you have to go to an expensive studio to have some dramatic affect created. But it does mean leave your pets, hobbies, unshaved face and messy hair at home! There was this guy who wanted to be a Director at an old established funeral home. His picture was of him dressed up like Luke Skywalker fighting Darth Vader with a light saber. Probably not the look the funeral home was looking for in their next director. Appearance is important, so make yourself look like the job in every aspect you possibly can.

Background Photo
Use a photo that will send a message you are on the job. If you are a petroleum engineer, maybe an oil field, a city planner, maybe a map of a community you planned, a nurse – stethoscopes. You get the idea. But whatever you choose do not let it be distracting or unprofessional.

You have just created your first impression. Step away from your profile for an hour or so. Come back and read it as if you were a recruiter or hiring manager and just pulled up your profile, what would you think? What message does it send? Hopefully that you are a professional and a friendly person people would like to work with. After all, nobody intentionally hires the qualified person that everybody hates! (Although we have seen evidence to the contrary!)

Summary
Now how about your summary? This will take a little more thought. Please put aside what you know about yourself for a moment. Go up to the LinkedIn search bar and search for the job title you have, had, or are hoping to land. Print out and read several job postings for which you would like to apply and that you are at least 80% qualified for. By that we mean you are an expert at 8 out of 10 of the requirements of the job. On the back of each one of the postings write down who they are looking for. Not so much what, but who.

Our Sales Manager is not a bad example, believe it or not. Notice, the description speaks to characteristics and qualities more that the technical how-to:

> *I was the Sales Manager for Oracle for fifteen years covering the ten western states. I managed 150 of the brightest sales professionals in the industry. By creating an analytical data base, actively listening to our customer needs and understanding the strengths and weakness of our many viable competitors I trained and led this talented team to the top. Together we met or exceeded every annual sales goal with an approximate average of 104% of our target. We were awarded the "Golden Hammer" by the CEO four times for being the top producing sales team in the company.*

This sounds more like the person. If the summary were full of *what's* it might include words like Sharepoint, Pipedrive sales tracking or CRM. These should appear in the achievement statements, but only if they are in the job postings, that is!

Here is another example, much shorter, from our industrial engineer:

> *An Industrial Engineer (IE) who thrives in a dynamic and challenging manufacturing environment. Proven track record of results using cutting-edge systems and processes toward exceeding expectations in Return on Investment, Delivery, Quality, and Cost Reduction.*

We could build the engineer out for another sentence or two, depending on the needs the employer expressed in the postings.

Write your summary and walk away from it for 30 minutes. Come back and read it and ask yourself this question: "Does this sound like the person in the job postings?" Note – Do not ask: Does this sound like me? With that said, if you have nailed this, then this is you. And it is the *you* the employer is looking for! Well done! Don't be afraid to continue to refine it as you go along. As you reread your summary be sure you have included the key words and phrases of your industry that the recruiter would be most likely to use in his/her search for the next employee. Please: not similar words or words that mean the same thing. Use the current industry words. Remember, recruiters, HR persons and search engines are *not* subject matter experts in your industry. So word recognition is a key factor here. Make it easy for them! This also demonstrates good written communications; to be able to write to your audience.

LinkedIn Profile Page
First thing: Get your picture in there! Next, for your current or most recent job, LinkedIn will pull your organization's name and your job title from the work experience section. So be sure it is 100% accurate. Remember, the new employer is very likely to call your past employer and make some inquiries. Let us dispel myth here: past employers can talk all they want about you as long as they tell the truth.

If you are working a temporary job outside of your field, that will not help you in your job search so leave it off. I have seen many white collar professionals work in retail or fast food restaurants to help pay the bills while looking for their next job. You will need to list that job on an application, but not on your LinkedIn profile – or resume, for that matter. Neither of these are job histories, they are to show your relevance and value in your field.

The *Education* field will populate from the most recent institution you attended. So, if you have an MBA from an Ivy League school, but subsequently you took a yoga class, don't show the yoga school or the MBA may be missed by a hurried recruiter. Make it easy for them!

Summary

This is dead easy and very critical. And you have already done it. Just copy and paste the summary you wrote in the last section. As a reminder, it must…

    1. …reflect the nature of the job postings you are looking at.

    2. …judiciously be filled with the key word and phrases in those postings. If it misses the key words and phrases, you will be missed by the recruiters' search. If you get that right, but your summary does not speak to the needs of employer (the employer's pain) and to the characteristics of their desired employee, they won't care about the key words. Remember way back in Chapter 4 we said there are some things that can be flexible. These are not them. You must be firmly committed to this.

Experience

Enter your work experience in reverse chronological order. Remember to keep all your job titles accurate. Almost. Yep, almost. This is where we can show a little flexibility. But you must be accurate and honest. If your title was Team Lead, put that in the corresponding space. But if you acted a lot like a Project Manager, enter your job title as Team Lead/Project Manager. Notice, I did not write *Project Manager*. You must have the Project Manager title and your PM certificate to say that. Another way to say it is, "Team Lead with Project Management Accountabilities." (*Accountabilities* is so much better than *Responsibilities*.)

Vice President can be a cryptic title. And there are lots of those around! If that is your entire title, please add something more meaningful and descriptive. Vice President/Operations and Facilities. Or Vice President Managing National Human Resources and Customer Service.

Don't forget, if you can use the same descriptor word as an adjective as are found in your job titles, *do it*! (Adjectives modify nouns. Unless you have a 5th grader, you may have forgotten that little bit of grammar.)

Languages

This is mostly straightforward. If you have any language skills, add them to your profile. Let's say you are born and raised as an English-speaking American. Please put English, Native or Bilingual Proficiency in your profile. Notice, LinkedIn does not ask for "foreign or additional" languages.

We like the way they do it. You free form your language and then choose the appropriate proficiency level: Native or Bilingual, Professional Working, Limited Working or Elementary proficiency. We are not sure exactly what "Elementary proficiency" means. But we can speak enough Spanish to order dinner and stay out of most Mexican jails; that may qualify!

What if the jobs you are looking at do not have a language requirement? Or your second or third languages are not commonly spoken in the area? Lance is a Native American-English speaker, and he also speaks, reads and writes French pretty well. He lives in Colorado where he may be the only French speaker! Add the language(s)! It shows a level of learning ability, well roundedness and – what if your interviewer speaks French?! This can be a good personal connection to make…and you are probably not in Colorado.

The most useful languages in North America are English (also the language of business in Europe and most of Asia), French and Spanish. Spanish-speaking immigrants are having a powerful impact on American businesses. Considering the United States does not have an "official language" and we come from such a diverse background, it is a wonder we do not have several commonly spoken languages.

If you are in Canada, French is the accepted language for a major portion of the population in and around the Province of Quebec. (That is where Lance learned my French by the way. Two rather distinct dialects and accents.) Has it ever helped him in my employment? Not really, but most employers find it impressive to some degree. We Americans who are not all that use to a true multi-lingual culture think that someone who can speak more than one language must be smart or a good learner. Both of which may help you in a job search.

The bottom line is this: include your language(s), they cannot hurt you. What do you think an employer is going to say when they see on Lance's LinkedIn profile that he speaks French? "Well this Lance guy looks pretty strong. But …. He speaks French, pass on him!" Or do you think they may say. "Lance has a good science education and background, the experience we are looking for, good endorsements, looks like he has done well at his previous jobs and he is probably pretty well rounded. He speaks a second language, he follows some art and literature on his Facebook, he is involved in the community and sports. He just might be our winning ticket. Bring him in, I want to talk to him."

Volunteer

A good thing to do here is: search for the companies you would like to work for on Twitter, Facebook and G+. You will often see company activities and the employees, (many of whom may be recruiters) volunteering for certain causes. They can be working on fun runs for the fight against birth defects or supporting children's hospitals, the fight against cancer etc. If you have any experience supporting or participating in any of the causes the employer is involved in, you know which ones to put first. But whatever and wherever you give back to the community, show it. Community involvement is very important to many employers.

One word of caution: Stay away from political and controversial issues. I know you believe in them as do I. But they are not appropriate in today's workplace and therefore are not appropriate in the job search. Lance recently had a job seeker in his office who was very much an environmentalist and was very vocal about ending all fracking operations. (A major industry here in Colorado.) And her social media activity showed that. She actually tried to get a job in an international oil company, who "fracks" here in Colorado and elsewhere, in their legal department no less! Really? Need we say more? And no, she did not land the job, for that matter, she did not even get an interview. No surprise there!

On the other hand, Lance knew a fellow who was interviewing for a position as the head trader at a prestigious wealth management firm here in Denver. When he interviewed with one of the partners and founders of the firm he noticed the Boy Scouts of America awards on the partner's wall. The applicant was an Eagle Scout in his youth. So he wisely asked about the Scout awards and found the partner very passionate about scouting. So when the partner finally took a breath Lance's guy said: "I love scouting too! I was fortunate enough to have parents who helped me earn my Eagle Scout award, and my wife and I have two boys in scouting today!" Ummm…let's see…guess who got the job? Yep, Lance's guy!

So if you can see a company or officer sees the value in a particular social or community event, and you can honestly make the connection … DO IT!

Following Groups and Companies
This part is the easiest and fastest part of all: You should be able to predict what to do here. These will reflect the companies and industry you work in. If a company you have identified to work for is following or participating in any groups, etc. you should be at the same party! You will find hiring managers, peers and even the golden recruiter right there in front of your eyeballs!

Lance was working with a Petroleum Engineer who was out of work for about a year. As he set up her LinkedIn and other social media sites, he discovered there is a plethora of petroleum engineer groups on all fronts! Who knew? Lance didn't, she didn't. Not at least until we looked for them. We quickly made connections at major and local companies, The Colorado Schools of Mines (*the* school for her industry, as it turns out). Many of the groups turned out to be very useful and soon she achieved her goal – getting The Job! – in a very competitive field. She obviously had what it took professionally, but now she was able to provide that information in a way that was meaningful to her target audience.

Endorsements
Endorsements have some value, but don't lose any brain cells over getting them. The value is limited for two reasons:

1. They can be sought after by every user and are also pushed to every user, and

2. Giving an endorsement is done with a single click.

With that said, please don't endorse anyone just because. If the endorsement is for "Leadership" you should really believe and be able to articulate why this person has Leadership qualities. That person will receive a notification of the endorsement and then be prompted to endorse you. So you will get endorsements. Recruiters do like to see a pattern of endorsements on your profile, but they also understand there is a limited value. Frankly, people have endorsed us for things which we don't have a clue about. Everyone on LinkedIn who is looking for employees knows this goes on.

Recommendations

Recommendations are a GOLD MINE! After looking at your summary, recruiters often go straight to your recommendations! They will skip right past your entire experience section to get to these!

What is a Recommendation? It is a short statement of about 100 words, given to you, demonstrating your value to the organization. And you cannot edit the recommendation. That is where the perceived value exists. You can request a fellow LinkedIn member to write one. You can decide if you want to show it or not on your profile. But you cannot write it or edit the endorsement. Recruiters see recommendations as an honest assessment of the value you brought to your employers, past and present.

You will want to seek out about six. This shows a pattern of who you are professionally and what you have added. You can certainly ask the writer of your recommendations to reference certain skills or accomplishments that are the most relevant to your current job search. Again, that is based on the job postings you are looking at. But do not write it for them. Each one needs to have its own unique style and verbiage.

Who do you ask for these? Easy! Supervisors, peers, direct reports where applicable, vendors and contractors. That way the recruits can get a 360-degree panorama of you.

Let's look at a couple Lance asked for from former clients, a co-worker and a colleague from a business competitor:

> Dr. Farr taught me excellent tools that I put to immediate use in searching for a new professional opportunity. The curriculum mixed with his balance of humor, seriousness, intensity, passion, and compassion made all the difference in making the experience one of the most rewarding and important steps at that point in my career. Very shortly after, I had much more success in my more focused search, was invited to more interviews, and had

multiple employment offers that exceeded my expectations. – Scott W., PhD. Engineer

For the past four years I have known Dr. Lance Farr. Lance is second-to-none in the areas of career coaching and counseling. Lance has offered insightful and meaningful career planning and job search advice. I will never forget Lance's coaching to prepare me for a salary negotiation. I have no hesitation to recommend Lance in the setting of career coaching and counseling. Please feel free to contact me for additional information and reference. – Richard O., attorney

Lance is a powerful presenter and has a great teaching style. He is effective in presenting complex topics and taking advantage of social media to make his point. He has a great classroom personality. It is a pleasure to be in one of his classes. – Tom F., former co-worker, now retired VP of Marketing for a major multinational (now collects root beer stuff)

Dr. Farr is an extremely knowledgeable and dynamic individual. He has expertise in the job search and networking market. I learned so much talking and working with him. – Business competitor

Yes, even a competitor. Maybe even *especially* a competitor!

Now if you were a recruiter looking for out-placement services or a training leader, these would likely speak to you. And the beauty is, Lance didn't have to write them!

And since we don't want Lance to get all the accolades in this chapter, here's a LinkedIn recommendation for Dan:

I was very fortunate to have an opportunity to work with and develop what is sure to be a lifelong friendship with Dan during my tenure at HRO. Dan is one of those individuals that you instantly connect with. He is not only very knowledgeable in all aspects of HR and personnel management but he has some great stories to share in which he shares his knowledge. He always makes time for those who need advice, support or good counsel.

I miss working closely with Dan every day but am thankful that we stay in touch and see each other on occasion. He is almost always the first person in the room that I want to say hello to. Dan is truly one of the GREAT people in this sometimes treacherous industry of HR + legal professionals! – Ann W. Director of Legal Recruiting (former co-worker)

Remember – seek out at least six references! Go out and get them.

The Job Market for Today checklist

_____ A good LinkedIn profile is critical to my success.

_____ If I have additional languages beyond English, be sure to include them.

_____ I should seek out LinkedIn recommendations from co-workers, supervisors, even some of my competitors.

_____ Endorsements are fine, but not nearly as powerful as recommendations.

_____ Join, follow and participate in groups that companies in which I am interested are participating.

_____ Include volunteer activities I am involved in, especially if the companies I want to work with are involved in those same activities.

Don't overlook the value of LinkedIn recommendations – seek them out.

7   LinkedIn – *The* Search Engine

With 44,000 jobs being added every second and well over 90% of recruiters on LinkedIn, it is not an exaggeration to say the site has rocketed to be *the* job market of today and the foreseeable future! Finding the jobs is easy business. But that will not be enough, will it? You already know how to make yourself look like the job. That is pretty straightforward. Finding job openings is as easy as typing the title of the job in the search box near the top of the page. No big deal there…actually it is rather fun to do. We just typed in *Project Manager in Denver* and came up with 3,452 results! That is actually too many, isn't it? Who wants to wade through all that?

So let's do some refining. After you make a search, and find out you are overwhelmed with the number of results, use the *Advanced* features on the left of the page. Dan tried *Project Manager Wells Fargo in Denver* and narrowed his results to four! He added his home zip code and came up with three. That is how you target a job and company on LinkedIn.

Networking

Now that we have three jobs to look at it, we really need to find some networking contacts. Preferably from our existing contacts, recruiters, HR or the hiring manager. All would be better than one. Which would you rather do: hit a home run or a grand slam? If you said "a home run will do," you are simply not as competitive as we are – and one of us might be your competition for this job. Then what? As one of our children say: "Second place is the first loser."

So multitask here. Go to LinkedIn and find a job. OK. Got it? Now choose the *View* function for this job. You are about to find very, very valuable information. When Lance did this on the Wells Fargo job, he was immediately shown two of his contacts working at Wells Fargo. Both came from his organization! That's good news right there! These may come from your contacts; groups you belong to or alumni from the same university. The more you are involved in LinkedIn the more likely you are to find these contacts. These are Lance's first two networking contacts. They may even get paid by their employer for recommending him, if he gets hired. Now they have some skin in the game as well. Yes, a good way to make new friends!

Lance's son and one of his sons-in-law are oil men. Both of their employers will pay them a bounty of 2,500 clams for recommending an employee who gets hired! The concept which makes it work is simple. The "boys" would like to bring a little extra cash home and they know if their recommended job candidate is not a viable option and won't get the job, they don't bother. The recruiter understands this as well. So he/she takes the recommendations seriously. The recruiter is happy, the new employee is happy, the boys are happy, their wives are happy, Lance is happy. They are all happy. So thank you for doing this!

Back to the Wells Fargo job now.

Lance also saw the details of the job, the exact job title, the job ID number, a description of the employer, a link to the company website for the application process and…drum roll please – and ten more similar jobs! Yes, ten more. Three jobs turned into thirteen jobs, just like that! Try that one on! Or as his dear sweet mother used to say: "Put that in your pipe and smoke it!" He was never sure what that meant or why she said it. They never smoked in his family. But it brings a smile to his face to say it.

Step One
Now make your connections. In this case simply e-mail your two contacts, let them know you will be applying for the Project Manager 4 position, Wholesale Loan Services, in the Denver office. In your e-mail to them, ask for two favors:

1. Do you know anyone in the department who I can have an informational interview about the position (preferably the hiring manager)?

2. Can I use their name on the application (that is: How would you like to make some extra scratch? Uhhh … a chance at some free money? Who would say no?).

Now we all know nothing is ever really free. So they owe you. Once your new-found friend retrieves you the names and contact information for an informational interview, you apply with his/her name, and let them know you did so. Then ask them to hand carry your resume to HR and the hiring manager. It is in his best financial interest to do so. Because you want your friend to say how you are a very good fit and will be a contributor from Day One. That is a simple *quid quo pro* and certainly is not asking too much. Plus, it helps ensure your friend collects the bounty.

You certainly must be asking but what if you do not have such an easy connection to make? Then proceed to step two.

Step Two
Go to either the search box at the top of the page or the *Key Word* search box at the side of the page. Who cares? They both seem to work the same. Now search for *Contacts who work for Wells Fargo*. When Lance did this, he found a total of 22 contacts this way. Now repeat step one. But what if you strike out on step two? Then go to step three.

Step Three
Use the same search boxes and search for:

1. Recruiters who work for Wells Fargo,

2. Human Resources who work for Wells Fargo,

3. Project Managers who work for Wells Fargo, and finally

4. People who work for Wells Fargo.

Whew. Hopefully you will not have to go that far. But if you do – *do it*. Being one of 200+ resumes and applications is yesterday's way. Live and play in today.

Now that you have taken about five minutes and found some names of people at the company you want to work for, start connecting with them. This is pretty simple. Click on *Connect*, which sends a generic request to this key player inviting them to connect to you and giving them the opportunity to look at your profile. What, you ask? Yes, if you have made your profile look like a Project Manager, or whatever your job field is, this recruiter is about to take a look at it! And guess what they will exclaim in utter joy? "This person (YOU) may well be the relief to my pain!" If so, expect a phone call. We have seen it happen many times. In fact, right in Lance's class on social media while we were building the profiles out! That is powerful stuff.

But in the meantime, if you do not get the instant phone call, do not be disheartened. We have just begun to have some fun here.

Step Four
Take this person's name and start searching for them on Twitter, G+ and the company's Facebook. Here is why:

Very recently, Lance was working with an attorney job seeker who wanted to work for a certain large brokerage firm in the compliance department. So they searched up the firm's name on the usual suspect places mentioned above. They found a recruiter for compliance officers on LinkedIn. They then searched the recruiter's name on Twitter and found her, then Facebook and found her on the company page volunteering. They reached out to her on all fronts and she connected to his client the same day! How sweet is that? And it took of all five minutes.

We will take a more detailed look at the other social media services shortly.

We have a friend who recently changed his executive position at one company for an executive position at another company. We asked how he did that, and he said he used LinkedIn exclusively to gain his new job. We asked him to explain what he did.

He told us it was simple. He was looking for a different challenge, so about a year before he left his job, he begin scouring LinkedIn for other individuals who held the same or similar positions at their company that he did in his, and he asked them to connect with him. He also found their bosses and connected with them. Once he had those connections, he hunted for the in-house recruiters at all those large companies and – you guessed it – he connected with them.

But that's not all he did. Next, he looked at the profiles of all those folks with whom he had connected to see what groups they were part of, and if he wasn't already a member of those groups, he joined them. And then he became a very active contributor to those groups. He weighed in on questions that were asked by members of the group. He posted articles that were relevant to the group, offered his opinions and asked for the opinions of others.

Several times during the months he did this, he was approached by recruiters, peers and even some of the peers' bosses to see if he was interested in considering their company as a place to work. Since he was not quite ready to make the move, he graciously declined.

Then the day came when he was ready to make a change. He posted that information on LinkedIn and in the groups he was a member of. Before the end of the day he had an invitation to interview, and within several days he had almost more invitations to interview than he could handle. So he was in the enviable position of being able to pick and choose where he wanted to go. He accepted a position in the same industry – for one of his competitors – at a higher position and at much higher pay.

We think you could call that a LinkedIn success!

Making other connections

You have learned how to make targeted connections on LinkedIn based on finding people involved in the companies and industries you want to work in. But there is another way to make less-targeted connections, and these do have some usefulness.

On the top tool bar right between *Profile* and *Jobs* is *My Network*. Try that. The drop down will have: *Connections, Add Contacts, People You May Know* and *Find Alumni.* I find *People You May Know* to be the most useful. The list that comes up is based on connections you have in common. At the bottom of each mini profile is *Connect.* Click on it. You just sent this person a connection request. If they know you they are likely to connect to you (presuming they like you that is!). If they do not know you, they will either ignore your connection request, accept it or maybe go to your profile page and check you out. In any case, you have invested little time and effort and will build your network this way. You can typically make three or four connections a day this way.

When you receive a connection request, don't be a snob. Accept them. You need a convincing reason not to accept one. You never know who is going to be the connecting point to your next job! Lance will tell you a true story about a grandma in a little bit.

Hint: Do you want to be really cool? On your LinkedIn Profile page, in your contact section will be the URL to your page. Use that to hyperlink on your resume, e-mail signature, Twitter, G+, Facebook and everything else you can think of. By doing so every time you are communicating with the world you are inviting the world to look at your LinkedIn page.

We suggest you make the top of your resume look something like this:

Dr. Lance Farr
Denver, CO   LinkedIn   303-123-9874
DrFarr@gmail.com

Nice and simple, creating more room in the body of the resume for valuable achievement statements. Note that both his LinkedIn and e-mail are hyperlinked (shown above by underlining). That way all anyone has to do is *control click* and they are on his LinkedIn profile page and sending him an e-mail invitation to a job interview. Remember, make it easy for them. And for the over-40 crowd who will experience age-based discrimination, this helps you show you are savvy and not out of date after all.

In addition to placing his LinkedIn hyperlink on his resume, Lance also includes it includes it in the signature line of his e-mail and he positions it to the left of his name. Unless you are reading Hebrew or Chinese, you read from left to right, and everybody reads top to bottom. So leverage that:

LinkedIn   Dr. Lance Farr

Well, this book is on social media job seeking but you got a freebee on resume, e-mail signatures and employer age discrimination as well. What a value!

We should make a preemptive defensive move here. We have intentionally not given you step-by-step, click-here instructions for LinkedIn. Simply because, as we all know, some webmaster or programmer will decide to move a button or rename a link or something. So, don't look for screen shot help here. Besides, in today's professional world, you MUST be at least that savvy. If you are not, start clicking and learning.

Review:

    1. LinkedIn is the job market

    2. Look like the job and an employee of the company

    3. Follow groups and participate

    4. Find individuals who can help you in those companies

    5. DO IT

The Search Engine for the Job Market for Today checklist

_____ Finding jobs on LinkedIn is much more powerful than I ever imagined!

_____ Finding contacts on LinkedIn at the companies I want to work in is much easier than I ever imagined!

_____ I should include a hyperlink to my LinkedIn profile on my resume.

_____ I need to poke and prod around on LinkedIn to learn for myself how to do many of the things Lance and Dan are pointing out.

_____ I will be using LinkedIn far more in my job search than I ever thought I would.

_____ I should include my LinkedIn hyperlink in the signature line of my e-mails.

8 Facebook

Facebook (FB) has become the standard for social media. Not only can you connect with people you actually know, also you can find old high school chums, neighbors and those you wish you had forgotten. Personally, we have never been sure what the real value of Facebook is. But that attitude may put us in the minority in today's world. There are, to be sure, several good uses for the job seeker that have germinated in this cyber world. And at least one very common use for the recruiter. In fact – you should know about it, because it is a potential deal breaker for you. So, no matter what your personal preferences towards Facebook are, pay attention!

Here is a MUST: Your Facebook must be so clean your Puritan ancestors would not be embarrassed. Seriously. That is not a joke. The major reasons recruiters and Human Resource personnel look at your Facebook, and they *will* look at it, is to judge what kind of person you are. That is, do they think you:

    1. will cause them a lawsuit and

    2. will you fit into the company culture?

It does not matter if you like this or not, if it is fair or not or you think it is an intrusion of your privacy. It is the way it is and there is no way around it. So, be smart. Leverage it to your benefit.

To do that it will be useful to know what employers are looking for, wouldn't it? Here are a few things that will cause serious issues for you if you venture down these lanes:

1. Negative comments about past or current employers. Even if they are true.

2. Pictures and or references of alcoholic beverages and controlled substances no matter how innocent or how legal.

3. Racist, sexist and intolerant comments and attitudes.

4. Comments and images of a sexual nature.

5. Extreme political and religious comments. (This is hard to define, but these are such subjective and changing views. Our suggestion is to stay away from them altogether.)

6. Poor grammar and writing along with a lack of creativity. We have yet to work with a job seeker who claims to have poor written and verbal communication skills. But in reality, very few have good ones. Facebook is where it shows. Or at least, that is the thinking here.

7. Your Facebook friends – and family...YES...NO!...Yes! It is true.

Let us explain:

Facebook friends and family members. Here is the thought: You get your home page and wall and feeds all nice and Puritan-like, right? Employers like it that way. But maybe you are just putting up a facade? What are you really like? You are like your friends and family! That is what you are really like. Trust us you are, whether you are or not. What we mean is, that is the assumption which will be made. And frankly, a perfectly reasonable one. It does not matter if it is true or if you like it. The reality it will bring to you if your site is not clean is one of…"Next applicant please." Not the reality we are looking for here.

On the other hand, if you turn all those assumptions on their heads, you are much more likely to get the interview. You should be making positive comments about the culture of current and former employers, how much you like what you do, modestly mention contributions, raises (not by amount silly rabbit) and promotions. Talk about the great people you work with and how valuable they are. Do you recall our Sales Manager example?

"...I managed 150 of the brightest sales professionals in the industry ... the strengths and weakness of our many viable competitors..."

Comments like these show your professionalism, good attitude and demonstrate you are a pleasure to work with, manage and know where your success comes from.

In short – you'll never be an HR problem for your employer.

On personal matters, stick with family and real friends. Talk about vacations, family activities, participating in community-improving events, helping the little old lady cross the street! Get it?

Unfriend anyone who could give the wrong impression to your would-be employer. Did we say would-be employer? How about your current employer? Yes, them too. There was a middle school teacher in town a few years ago who posted a picture of her holding a martini glass with the sun setting in the background. A very nice photo. She was on a vacation during the summer and was apparently sharing her vacation via Facebook. Her employer, a public school district, saw the photograph and fired her on the premise she was encouraging her middle school students to use controlled substances. She appealed the termination and lost. Yep, she lost.

And she's not alone – scarcely a month goes by that you don't read about someone who was fired because they were unwise in what they posted on Facebook. Shortly before this book was published, there was a highly publicized Facebook firing when a young woman announced on Facebook that she was starting a new job at a local daycare center. Unfortunately she added that she really hated working with children, but it was a job, so she had accepted it.

One of her "friends" (hopefully not a member of her family!) called her Facebook post to the attention of the daycare center owners, and they reached out to her to let her know it was no longer necessary to show up for work the next day – she was fired before she even started her new job!

So – please believe us when we say be very cautious about what you post on your Facebook pages. The lesson to be learned: Get your Facebook Puritan clean and keep it that way. The fewer times you file for unemployment the

Be careful what you, your friends and family post on Facebook!

happier your life will be. If you are worried about offending your Facebook friends, ask them if they will pay your bills while you are looking for a job.

Now, lest we be accused of being FB haters, here are some very important uses of FB:

Nearly every company has a Facebook page. How many is that? Well about fifteen million businesses, companies and organizations. They use it for one or more of several good reasons. These would be advertising products and services, customer feedback both positive and negative and for showcasing their community involvement. That is – what is important to them? In addition, there are about 25 million small businesses on Facebook.

So why should you care? If you care about the same community events of your next employer, don't you think you should be involved *and* put it on your Facebook page? Also, remember our experience with the job seeker looking for work as a compliance officer in Chapter 7? Sometimes you can even see the involved person's name on Facebook. When that happens, look for them in LinkedIn and Twitter. Follow them, their causes, their employers and for heaven's sake, connect with them.

Is this the end of it? Nope. Many companies advertise job openings on Facebook. How about that? Did you know that? Good for you if you did. How would you like to sit down in your next job interview with the person you have been following on Facebook, Twitter and LinkedIn? It would be as if you almost knew him/her. Your anxiety level will go way down and you will interview better. When you are asked "Why do you want to work for this company?" Or "Why should we hire you?" You can say "Well for two major reasons. One is, as I hope I have been able to demonstrate today, I have the specific skill set and experiences you are looking for." (Remember, you gave specific achievement statements as answers to questions, so as to remove all doubt about your abilities to do the job well.) "And, I have noticed your organization is very involved with Habitat for Humanity (or whatever it is). That is something near to my heart. I really have enjoyed working on the projects and have made good friends there as well. So I am confident I will not only be a contributor to the bottom line from the very beginning, but that I will also fit into your company culture as well."

Is this important? Let me tell you about the conversation that does not happen as part of the hiring decision: "Well, Lance has the skills we are looking for, but he'll never fit in and I just don't think he is a good fit. OK then, let's hire him!" But the one that *does* happen frequently is: "(Insert your name here) doesn't have all the skills we are looking for, but I really like him and I think he will fit into the company well. I think he will be able to shorten the learning curve and be up to speed soon. OK, let's hire him!" Does that answer your question if connecting to and understanding the company on Facebook is important?

If you want more reasons, try the 2014 Jobvite Recruiting Survey: 93% of hiring managers will review a candidate's social media profile as part of their hiring decision; 55% have reconsidered based on what they find with 61% of those reconsiderations being negative and 39% positive. This same survey said 65% of recruiters say volunteering or donating to charities gives a positive impression. So like we said: leverage Facebook properly, reflecting the needs, attitudes and culture of the companies you're interested in. By doing this you will have a leg up on over half of the competition.

Networking on Facebook
Facebook has a ready and willing network for you: your friends. Simply prepare a summary, yes based on those six job postings, and put it on your timeline. Add a little ditty in front of it like: "Hey friends. I am looking for a new position and I am not sure you are well acquainted with what I have been doing. So here is a short summary. If you know anyone in my field, would you pass this along to them? Thanks!"

Now, guess what you are going to add to the bottom of your summary? The link to your LinkedIn page!! How many people have you just notified and invited to see your LinkedIn profile? Hundreds if not more. And as they share it, how many more? If you have been friending and following industry contacts and groups, you have invited key decision makers and people in the know to look at and share your LinkedIn profile. Even if they do not have a job for you, it is not at all uncommon for these key players to either share your request with their contacts and/or give you some ideas. I have seen it happen. It confirms the goodness and caring of humanity.

You never know where the contact will come from. Lance had a job seeker in his office in the height of the recession when unemployment was double digits and still growing. His particular field was really hurting. Lance told him to notify everyone he could, just like above. His grandmother in Wisconsin (which was hit much harder than Colorado by unemployment at the time) responded to his request by saying: "You have a cousin out here you don't really know. I think he is in the same field. Why don't you contact him?"

So he did and the cousin forwarded our job seeker's information to his boss. His boss decided if those two cousins were anything alike, he wanted to speak to him. So he flew our job seeker out from Denver to Wisconsin for an interview. Not only was he interviewed, but he was offered a job the same day! So if you live in Wisconsin and you were beat by some cowboy from Colorado…Sorry…well not really. It is a competitive, harsh world. And all you have to do is show it that you really are good. This guy did it, and beat the odds on doing it. (P.S. Thanks, Grandma!)

Facebook checklist

_____ Facebook isn't just for whiling away the time – I can use it for my job searches.

_____ Make sure my Facebook page is Puritan clean!

_____ Be aware of the posts friends and family place on Facebook!

_____ Never post negative items about my current or former employers.

_____ Use Facebook to post some of my accomplishments.

_____ Follow companies and find out what community projects they are involved in.

Stay Positive!

Okay – what we've covered so far in social media is a lot, so let's take a slight change of pace and talk about something a little more…fluffy…now.

When Dan was first laid off during the Great Recession, he attended a job search session offered by his church – ironically, or perhaps providentially, the class was taught by the man who is now his good friend and co-author: Dr. Lance Farr! One of the things that struck Dan was a discussion they had about the wide-ranging emotions associated with having lost a job, including relief, shock, denial, self-isolation, anger, remorse, guilt, panic, depression, resignation, acceptance, optimism and elation. (Any of those emotions sound familiar?)

Lance hastened to point out that these emotions weren't necessarily sequential, and you might leap ahead (to optimism and elation when you get an interview) or fall back (to resignation or panic when you hear you didn't get the job).

We have several friends who have been unemployed for long periods of time – years. Based on our working with them, we'd say these emotions are emotions each of them has experienced at one time or another in their job hunt. Dan is by nature a very optimistic person, so he didn't experience some of the more difficult emotions listed here – depression and panic. But he did find himself needing to fight many of the more negative emotions.

So – be prepared for a wide range of feelings, and map a strategy to deal with the difficult situation you are facing.

You have already started doing that through the pages of this book. You are taking the first steps to placing yourself in the Land of the Employed once again: you're learning how to attack this challenge that has come your way.

One of your most valuable tools in your job hunt will be the ability to remain positive. Hundreds of books and articles have been written on the power of positive thinking, and you need to believe every one of them!

Dan has developed ten keys to staying positive during this trying time in your life, so this chapter will be written from Dan's perspective (so when your read "I" know that this is Dan speaking!). Let's see if you agree with them:

Key #1 – Keep Busy
One of the best things you can do to ward off depression is to keep busy. Prepare for battle, launch your resumes and cover letters into the great unknown at an unprecedented pace. Don't fire without targets, and don't fire ill-prepared ammunition. You need to plan your attack, prepare your weapons (your resume, cover letter and LinkedIn profile) and identify companies for whom you are qualified to work. Plan how you will get resume screeners to put your resume in the Call-for-an-Interview pile. Some of the techniques we have been talking about will help with that.

Key #2 – Start an Exercise Program
Exercise is a great tool to battle depression. Select a time during the day that you will exercise, and stick to that schedule. Some people are morning people, and early mornings are a great time to exercise. However – you have to know yourself well. I know, for example, that any exercise program I start in the early morning hours is doomed to failure. I am one of those people that, if I was the one making the rules, I would say early morning meetings would be held at 10:00am or 10:30am in the morning. 5:00 only occurs once a day on my clock, and it is followed shortly thereafter by sunset.

I'd suggest exercising at least five, if not six days per week. I am a big believer in Sunday being a day of rest, and that makes sense for my exercising muscles too. The exercise I chose was to walk daily, Monday through Saturday.

Key #3 – Change Your Mindset
Surprisingly, this was one of the more difficult aspects of the job search for me. Prior to my lay off, we were pretty comfortable financially. We could

buy things more or less at whim (within reason, of course. We couldn't, for example, buy the Dodgers when they were for sale…). I am a book fiend, and buy many books each year. Twenty minutes on Amazon.com and I could easily drop $200 or more, and this sometimes happened several times each month. I found I could no longer do that – I needed to shepherd my resources. I became a coupon clipper for the first time in my life.

This was a hard adjustment to make. Frankly, it was probably a good adjustment to make, as on a monthly basis, we were seeing hundreds of dollars slip out of our budget for non-essential items. Once I finally got my mindset changed, it was easy to do. But the first little while it was difficult.

Key #4 – Marshal Your Resources

Immediately upon your change of employment status, determine what resources are available to you. What cash reserves do you have? If you needed to cash in a portion of your 401(k), could you? What revenues are coming in and what expenses demand payment? In a severe pinch, could a family member help out?

Are there expenses you can do without? Our home phone, internet and cable TV bill is close to $200 per month. We have cell phones, so we could certainly do without the cable TV and our home phone. That would save us a chunk of change. (We'd still need our Internet for job searching.) Do you have similar expenses? Are there corners you can cut? I have a friend who lost his job in May, and immediately sold his ski boat. He figured if he waited until the end of the water skiing season, he might be unable to sell the boat, or if he was able to sell it, he'd have to take less money for it. He traded in his wife's BMW for a car that was still functional but much less expensive. He economized.

You may want to look for something part-time to do to make ends meet. If you do that, be careful not to accept so many hours that you cannot conduct an effective job search. I've a friend who worked part-time for a moving company during his period of unemployment, and that allowed him the flexibility to work around the times he had set for his job search. Uber might be another option for you – you are 100% in control of your hours with that company.

You have children in college with large tuition payments due? Rather than pay those tuition expenses out of your savings, consider getting student loans. Even if you don't want your children saddled with those debts once they get out of college, you can still do that. Just have the understanding that you will make the loan payments when the time comes.

We stopped going out to eat. Whereas we were going out to eat once or twice a week, we curtailed that expense and saved plenty.

One of the first things I did was figure out the maze of requirements to apply for unemployment benefits, and did so. Depending on the state you live in, it often takes six weeks or so for unemployment benefits to kick in.

Key #5 – Remember: You're not alone

If you are unemployed in America, you share that stage with millions of Americans. Even though the unemployment rate reported by the government is just south of 5%, a LOT of people are out of work right now, many of them through no fault of their own. Good people are hitting the streets. Unfortunately, you are one of those good people.

While the saying goes, *Misery loves company*, that's not my point. My point is that you have not been singled out as the only one to lose his or her job. Keep the proper perspective: you and millions of other outstanding people

Remember – I am not alone!

– top performers, bright (even brilliant) people, innovators, hard workers, etc., have lost their job. Okay, that's a fact. But don't dwell on your loss so much that you miss opportunities that may be open to you.

Key #6 – Don't Be a Victim

I think this is an important consideration. What happened, happened. Don't waste your time blaming others, wondering how on earth management could have made that decision to let you go, etc. Sometimes that negative thinking comes through in your cover letters, and often even in your job interviews. You cannot afford for that to happen. Negativity is not a sought-after characteristic by employers and recruiters.

Near the end of my job search, it came to light that some companies in the United States were advertising that the unemployed need not apply, that they were only seeking currently employed applicants. I figure this must have seemed like a good idea to someone (probably someone who had never been unemployed – who may well be soon!), but they didn't pause to consider the public relations nightmare it would be for their company. What a short-sighted, mean-spirited approach to hiring.

Don't let those comments bother you. There will always be mean-spirited people like that in every walk of life, and I suppose VPs of Human Resources are no different – some can be like that. Who cares? To be honest, I wouldn't want to work for a company that treated people like that anyway!

As a hiring manager, I understood clearly that with the ups and downs of the economy in recent years, there was a great deal of outstanding talent on the outside looking in. Of course I needed to do my due diligence when interviewing someone who had been laid off: asking them why they were let go, checking references, etc. But if I liked you as a candidate and you weren't currently employed, it was a bonus for me: that meant you could start the next day, and I wouldn't have to wait for you to give two weeks' notice, then run the risk of your current company countering my offer, etc. It is a win-win situation for all of us!

Key #7 – Set a Schedule
I think if you are busy doing something productive with your time, the time will pass quickly, you won't sit around and brood or worry about your unemployed status, etc. Your job now is to find a job, and you should set a schedule that will enable you to search with a well-defined mission in mind: *Get That Job!*

Key #8 – Get Plenty of Sleep
Getting plenty of sleep is important, as it will help you deal with the depression and self-defeating doubts that might creep in occasionally. One of the best bits of advice I received at the time of my lay-off was to get good, consistent sleep. Occasionally I stayed up way later than normal, but generally speaking, I was in bed most nights by 10:00pm and arose most mornings by 7:00am.

Key #9 – Prepare for the Long Haul

At the time of this writing, our economy is improving somewhat. But it is so fragile. An unexpected jobs report, a lower earnings (or loss) report of a Fortune 200 company, unrest in the Middle East and a host of other such calamities (or risks of calamity) can cause the economy to reel and step back a few paces.

Experts reportedly claim that it takes a month of job searching for every $10,000 of income you are trying to replace. So, if you're trying to find a $70,000 job, plan on being out of work seven months. The first time I heard that the economy was strong, so it may even take more time to find a job in this New Economy.

Set your expectations appropriately, or you risk being disappointed. If you feel you'll be employed in two weeks, you may be disappointed. The key is to work as though you will be able to be employed in two weeks if you work hard, but be realistic in the expectation that it may take longer than that to become employed.

Statistics show the average worker who is laid off can expect a 25% to 40% cut in pay when s/he does go back to work. In my case, I took a 33% cut in pay when I returned to work, so I'd have to say that statement is pretty accurate – I am a pretty average guy. I have known a few who actually increased their pay, but mostly my friends and acquaintances have reported a loss of earnings when returning to work.

Key #10 – Build in some Entertainment

All work and no play makes Jack (and Jill) a dull boy (and girl). Make some time for yourself. Make time for your family – remember, everyone who loves you and in particular those who live under the same roof is sharing this experience with you, in one way or another.

When I told my mother I had been laid off, she said, referring to our two oldest children: "Oh, this would be a great time for you to go visit Katie in Chicago and Michael in Portland." I said yes, if it weren't for the need to be cautious with our monies at this time. Of course it would be unwise to take that round-the-world trip you've always wanted to take, or pack up the kids and head for Disney World.

But, depending on where you live, a drive in the mountains or a trip to the nearby ocean to see the sunset are inexpensive ways to spend time together and get out of the house. Perhaps a trip to the mall as a family, looking for the most outrageous window display you can find would keep everyone's spirits up. Or just a picnic in the park. We like Redbox movies – even on a tightened-belt budget we feel we can afford to rent a movie or two at Redbox. Whatever it takes, don't allow yourself to slip into the doldrums.

Key #11 – Hang in There!

Finally, hang in there. This time in your life will be over sooner than you think. Hopefully in the future as you look back on this experience, you can do so with introspection and insight, perhaps even fondness. It is easy to be professional when everything is going your way. But real professionalism manifests itself during adversity.

(You'll note I said I had ten keys, but provided eleven. Well, I am a firm believer in not over-committing, and in always providing more than promised....)

Stay Positive! checklist

_____ Stay positive – I must guard against negativity in my job search.

_____ Don't be a victim.

_____ Start an exercise program.

_____ Consider the feelings of my family – they are sharing my unemployment. Make time for them, and for entertainment with them.

_____ I am not alone -- millions of others are out of work.

_____ Set a schedule – including getting plenty of sleep.

10   Twitter and G+

Twitter seems to be a social networking phenomenon that has risen in importance in recent years. It's a way of sharing short, quick bites of information – cleverly called tweets – with friends and colleagues (tweeple). Since Twitter limits messages to 140 characters, you don't have to worry about people going on and on (like they can on Facebook, for example!). Some might be tempted to dismiss Twitter because of the brevity of the messaging. After all, how much important information can just a few characters provide?

If you are among those who question the value of short messages, consider the following:

> "I only regret that I have but one life to give for my country."
> – Nathan Hale (74 characters)

> "Give me liberty or give me death." – Patrick Henry (48 characters)

> "That's one small step for man, one giant leap for mankind." – Neil Armstrong (74 characters)

> "Never was so much owed by so many to so few." – Winston Churchill (62 characters)

As well as the following:

> "I am not a crook." – Richard M. Nixon (35 characters)

"I did not have sexual relations with that woman." – William Jefferson Clinton (66 characters)

"Read my lips – no new taxes." – George H. W. Bush (47 characters)

"A crude and disgusting video sparked outrage throughout the Muslim world." – Barack Hussein Obama (95 characters)

So now that you are convinced that 140 characters can convey powerful messaging – for good or ill – let's talk a little more about Twitter as a tool in your job search arsenal.

As with LinkedIn and Facebook, you have the opportunity to add many individuals – friends, colleagues, vendors, etc., to the network you can use for your job search. You can let your Lists (your Twitter network) know you are out of work, what kind of job you are seeking, or about an upcoming interview with a company.

Twitter is powerful despite few characters!

For many people, Twitter is a bit of a conundrum. It is easy to understand why. So many entertainers, politicians and professional athletes use it for either their own purposes or to yell at each other that they obscure the really good uses of it.

Here are some interesting facts about Twitter:
- There are about 100 million daily log-ins

- 1.3 billion registered users

- 320 million daily users

- 83 % of the Fortune 500 companies operate official company Twitter accounts (DMR Digital Stats and Gadgets, Craig Smith)

So what is Twitter and how do we leverage it?

Twitter is a micro blog, sort of instant messaging on steroids, allowing users to send short messages directly to handheld devices, wrist-worn devices, laptops and personal computers. Even though each Tweet must be fewer than 140 characters, your user's profile can contain much more, including pictures and videos. In fact, you can even tweet pictures, videos and images. With a little cleverness you could tweet your resume as an image! Getting interested yet? You should be, by the time we are done here you will see it is the notification system that every job seeker should be leveraging!

We will start at the top:

Your Twitter Profile
Your **photograph** can contain a picture within a picture. Use the same picture of you as you did on your LinkedIn profile. The background picture should also be the same. People are very visual animals and you want to build on that. You can actually start to build a sense of familiarity this way. (Recognition and reminders are important in building a sense of familiarity.) Even if your interviewer only sees a picture of you one time, when you walk into his or her office for the first time, they will experience a feeling of: "I know or recognize this person." Because they have invited you in for an interview, they must believe you are the answer to their pain points. They may even begin to recall your very impressive LinkedIn, Twitter and Facebook profiles along with your blog or other online portfolios and community involvement. They will no longer wonder if you can do the job, just if you are as good as you say you are. So interview well! Be friendly, conversational and speak to the resolution of their pain points. (We keep giving you pointers for interviewing, don't we?)

A picture *is* worth a thousand words, especially when the words demonstrate your expertise in the industry and match what the employer is looking for!

Next:

You need to first create your **Twitter tag line** (that is, who are you?). You are not an adorable person who loves to play with cats and enjoys long walks in the rain and listens to Billy Joel! Your Twitter tag line needs to be directed at who you are professionally. So simply write a summary of you based on the needs of the six job postings you searched out earlier in the book. You can do some rewording if you think it is too repetitive. But don't change it too much. Sending a mixed message could well spoil your opportunities for interviewing. It also does not demonstrate good written communication skills. Remember our little rant about written communications? Well, we don't really rant, we just want you to do well.

Next is a spot for your URL. Anyone want to guess which URL goes in there? Who said your LinkedIn profile? Good job, buy yourself a candy bar, you are on your way! We always want to be inviting everyone to view your LinkedIn profile at every opportunity.

You can skip your birthday, especially if it was as long ago as ours. No sense inviting age-based bias: too old or too young. Besides, it is not a job qualifier, so don't bother.

And that is the end of your Twitter profile – a nice and easy five-minute process. Go do it and come back.

Now let's look at the *Search Twitter* function. At this writing it is in the upper left of your screen.

What can you search for?

Jobs. Yes, jobs are posted on Twitter by both companies and professional recruiters! We just found jobs for Wireline Engineers in Colorado. Right now with oil at $25 a barrel those jobs are very hard to find. But if you like to blow things up 25,000 feet underground, this is the job for you! (Lance's son does this and he loves it!)

So go try it, and start with your exact job title, then use your field or industry. Not every company calls your job by the same name. *Wireline engineer* yielded jobs that *Wireline services* did not. But you can apply for jobs using both names. You have a perfectly good thinker, go ahead and think with it. You are an expert in your industry, not me!

In the Twitter job search you will undoubtedly find many companies you could work for. Do a couple things here -- follow them, and search for people who work at (insert the company name here) and follow them.

Next search for recruiters in your field. Use a little imagination here. Searching for *petroleum recruiters* rendered different results than *oil field recruiters*, which was yet different than *Wireline services recruiters*.

Follow them all. Each recruiter you follow will get a notification that you are now following them, and they may well go to your Twitter profile and see you are a job seeker and check you out! It only takes a moment for them to do it…and guess what? They will see the link to your LinkedIn Profile! Gotta love this stuff.

Here is one of the most valuable uses of Twitter for the job seeker. In the next chapter you are going to learn the importance of online portfolios and blogging in your job search. Twitter, perhaps the most powerful electronic notification system there is, will be how you will notify all these key players about your posts and portfolios. It makes it easy for them to see your value. So connect with as many individuals, companies and groups as you can. Retweets will get you around the world in about 80 nanoseconds!

Now a few words about **G+**.

G+ stands for Google, plus you. Kind of clever, I think.

G+ is an app you add to your standard Google account. It looks a little like Facebook and a little like Twitter. But it is neither. It has its own space and is a good tool for you to use.

Your G+ profile is pulled from your Google account. So if you don't have one, we suggest you get one – it's free. Again, make this profile picture and send the same message as your LinkedIn and Twitter profiles do.

You will notice the feed on G+ is full of pictures, messages and videos. These will come from those people and organizations you told Google you are interested in as well as those who you follow and who are following you. So the picture should be starting to form here. Search Google + for the contacts, companies, groups and recruiters who are important to you.

Believe it or not, you will most likely find new ones. By the way, yes, search for jobs also. Use all the same techniques we have been using. They will yield varying, but good, results.

Now there is more to this good stuff. Similar to Twitter, Facebook and LinkedIn, you can join communities based on your profession. You will see and can post far more information with each strike of the enter key on your keyboard using G+ than you are able to on Twitter or LinkedIn. And it tends to be more "friendly," that is, more informal than LinkedIn. So it is a very good space to connect with people, company causes and to contribute your expertise to the conversation. Yes, this is the place to really start.

So far, your social media presence has been mostly encouraging key players to come look at you. Not a lot of interaction. This is where that starts to change; we are going to throw a dynamic curve ball here, designed to create a two-way communication on the most important subjects to these employers. One of which will be lucky enough to be your next employer.

What is important to this lucky employer? Their pain points and whatever community concerns they are involved in. You will learn what those are from G+, Twitter and Facebook. Companies like to brag about theie community involvement a bit. Show they are not all like Daddy Warbucks.

Now that you know what is important to the employer and have joined their communities, start adding insightful commentary. The professional communities – those based on your industry – will give you ample opportunity to show how you have approached and solved many of the difficulties they are facing.

We just looked at an Interior Design community and found a company who "ensures your interior space meets your taste, need and benefit..." What an opportunity for you (if you are an interior designer) to post a picture of your work and tell a short story of how you meet your client's needs. (This sounds strangely like an achievement statement with a picture, doesn't it?) Not only is this company going to see your work, so will everyone else on your feed. Now ... Tweet it out!!!! How many more important people just saw it? Put it on Facebook....it is easy to have over a thousand people see it in just a few seconds. Hopefully you are starting to see the power and value of social media for the job seeker.

One of the features of G+ we really like is **Circles**. These are really e-mail lists of people and communities. Currently on the left upper portion of the G+ home page is a drop-down menu titled *Home*. Click on that and you will see about seven options. These include *profile, people, collections*, etc. By selecting *people*, you will be directed to a page full them. You can also search for individuals, communities and even add your e-mail contacts. When you select any of these people, companies or communities you will have the choice of creating a "circle" for them or adding them to an existing one. So you may want to put everyone you will be contacting in your job search into one circle. It just makes it easier. Search for all the people you have found so far in your quest for employment.

Now when you post that interior design photo and achievement statement, don't just put it on your G+ page and notify the one company. Share it with all your new G+ friends! Google has made it really simple. To post, you click on the appropriate icon for text, photo, link, video, event or poll. Add whatever you are going to add, then select the choice at the bottom of the window! You just sent a notification to all those people and added it to the G+ home page for all to see! So make it worth their time and they will continue to look at and respond to your posts. Like Twitter, they can re-share it with others. So your potential audience is massive. You will know if you are doing both Twitter and G+ right, because your audience will continue to grow. Remember, it only took Lance a couple of weeks to have the industry giants following him and to become the #8 search result on the Google search for "Scuba."

Another good Google function is *job searching*. You can be creative here. Searching by the company name, job title, industry and location all work pretty well. The reason we say "pretty well" is based on the fact that job posting is not a major target for G+. With that said, we have been able to find either many actual job postings or links to the postings on company web pages. One benefit of searching G+ is finding a networking contact simultaneously. Please do not overlook this resource, never close a door on possibilities.

Twitter and G+ checklist
_____ Twitter is a tool to lure people to my LinkedIn profile!

_____ I should follow companies, recruiters, HR people.

_____ Jobs are listed on Twitter.

_____ Recruiters follow candidates on Twitter.

_____ Google+ has a lot more potential to assist me in my job search than I ever imagined!

_____ G+ Circles = e-mail lists of people and communities.

Showcase Your Expertise

This chapter is where you learn to really showcase your expertise. We cannot think of a better way to show your industry knowledge, creativity, written communication skill and demonstrate your passion for your beloved profession.

There are several platforms to do this with. Choosing one or more to fit your industry and needs is up to your professional judgment. After all, you are the expert. For Lance's scuba experiment, he chose Google Blogger and Shutterfly photo sharing sites. But there are many other sites that are also free and may suit your needs better. Simply Google free blog sites, free photo sharing sites, free websites, etc.

We will start by looking at **Google Blogger**. It is part of the whole G+ thing. Just click on the *App* icon in the upper right corner of your Google page. It is nine small squares and looks a little like a tic-tac-toe game board. All your standard Google apps will be there. So choose Blogger and let the games begin!

One of the first things you will be asked is to name your blog. Be smart here. Use your name if possible. For example, Lance's was "Farr Better Scuba Instruction." It was unique and instantly he had it! Second is the e-mail address. Follow the same concepts as with all your professional sites. Remember the whole "SleepingWithTheBoss@..." e-mail thing? Still not a good idea here. Third – choose a template. Don't kill any stem cells here. Templates are super easy to change at any time, even after your blog is up and running. I suggest trying the "Simple" template. Chances are it will work great for you. Did you do it? If not, rather than just read about it here, take a few minutes and *do it*.

You are now the proud owner of a blog. That was easy and painless. Now design it. Designing it is largely a matter of experimenting. I found it very entertaining to do, so much so I have done several since. Some for family and some for the pure fun of it.

To design it find the *Layout* link on the left side of the page. Yep, choose it. There is the basic layout. There you will have the *Navbar, Sidebars, Header, Cross Column, Main* and *Footers*. Across the top are your basic edit functions: *Create a New Post, View Posts, View Blog, Save Arrangement, Preview, Clear* and of course the sprocket-looking *Settings* icon. Most of these are pretty self-explanatory. Click on *View Blog* and see what pops up in a new tab. Your blog! Did you see the title of your blog? Pretty cool and pretty empty right now. But don't close that tab. Leave it open and go back to the *Blog Design* tab.

Have a little fun and get ahead of yourself here for a moment. Choose the *Create a New Post* icon in the upper left corner. It looks like a pencil. Well, it does at the time of this writing. Enter a catchy title and write a few short sentences – on anything. Once you do that, go to the other tab so you can see your actual blog.

Notice any difference? Nope, you don't. This is not a streaming site. So simply refresh the blog page by either pressing the F5 key or clicking on the refresh icon on your browser. Now there it is! Very cool. I brought you through this exercise to demonstrate how easy it is to blog and our favorite way to build a blog. Which is: Every time you make a change to your blog during the design phase go to this tab and refresh it. And presto, nothing up our sleeve (that's English for *voilà*) you can see your change. If you like what you have done go and make the next change. If you don't, go back to the design page and change it. It is real fast and easy to go back and forth between the tabs. Let's try one on for size.

Back to your *Design* tab. You should be in *Layout*. On your navbar click on *edit* and choose a color. Click *Save* on the bottom. Now go to the blog tab and refresh the page. Like it? Keep it. Don't like it? Change it. Fast, fun and easy. Be careful, blogging can be habit forming. I really want you finding The Job, That Job. But…you may as well enjoy doing it!

Do the same with the header.

On the cross column we can really have some fun. Click on the edit function. Notice a few things here. You have a *Title* box. This is where we get clever. It is the place to put the name of your online portfolio or website. Lance's is "Class Photos." Underneath that is *Add external link*. The link he added goes to Shutterfly where the viewer can see dozens of photos organized by scuba specialty. There is one page for Open Water Diver (Beginning Diver), Advanced, Wreck Diving, etc., etc., etc. So now the viewer can see his students in and above the water having a great time, there are many pictures of the beautiful underwater world and tropical locations. Just thinking about it makes us want to stop writing and go play! Do you see the point here? Showcase what you have done for previous employers in a meaningful way to your next employer. You don't have to describe it in an interview for the employer to experience it. That is powerful.

Time to look at the sidebars. They have an interesting phrase in them. "Add a gadget." So click on *Add a Gadget* and you will get a pop up with over two dozen gadgets to choose from. The ones I think are the most valuable for you are: add a link (*LinkedIn, Twitter, Facebook* go here), *Followers, Blog Archive, Share It* and *Search this Blog*. Add some and see what happens. If you like it, keep it; if not – change it. Change it today or a year from now. It is that simple. Notice you can drag and drop the order of these, making it very easy to arrange them the way which suits you best.

In the side-bar-right-2-1 and 2-2 Lance added images: *Subscribe To, +1 Button* and *Google + Badge*. The more you can get people to interact with this site the higher it will come up on searches. The same is true for your LinkedIn account; the more traffic on it the more relevant it is to search engines.

Once you have the layout where you want it, you are ready to start posting. So here are some very important words about your post:

Blog post must-haves
- Be relevant to the would-be employer's needs

- College level "A" work

- Start with a thesis (Tell them what you are going to tell them)

• Explore each topic in the thesis in the order presented in the thesis

• Make all proper citations to your work

• Conclusion statement at the end

• Grammatically perfect (we live by spell and grammar checks)

Flexible stuff

• Add images, graphs, a bit of humor etc. to keep it interesting and let your personality show

You can break longer or more complicated posts into multiple posts. The first post Lance did on his scuba blog was a three-part post discussing the theories and aspects of dive physiology and decompression theory. He included charts, graphs and equations. (This is a subject he has published on before in textbooks.) He sent it to thirteen former students without any warning at all. Within 24 hours it had been re-shared across North America and Western Europe. It helped establish Lance as an expert in the field. He followed this post with a lighthearted one, "An Apple a Day, Healthy Habits for Diving." So some of his posts were pretty heavy-duty science of decompression theory while others were lighthearted or about fitness for scuba divers, others on advanced fin kicks for technical divers and more. All showcasing his expertise and experience as an Advanced Scuba instructor.

Here is an idea Lance found which really drove up his views. On occasion add an additional page with a good recipe for a delicious treat. Everybody likes those! His two most popular were Root Beer Float Cookies and Tortilla Soup! Here is how it worked. He had followers all over the world at this point throughout the entire industry reading all that stuff he had bloggd about. Then all of a sudden, here comes Root Beer Float Cookies. Who doesn't want to get that? So it was hit fast and hard from all angles and shared and re-tweeted like crazy! He could literally watch his audience grow. Not only was it fun to share, a whole new group of people saw his blog. What that means for you is more people and potential employers seeing your best work and being invited to view your LinkedIn profile! Plus, they see you are fun to have in the office! Pretty clever!

I can create my own
blog to showcase
my talents.

Sharing the blog

Once you get your blog up and going, post five or six articles. Start a little track record here. In the meantime you should have been building up your contacts in G+, LinkedIn, Twitter and Facebook. Now you are ready to blast them all with your expertise. You will have noticed at the bottom of each blog post are gadgets to do this with. We call them "blast gadgets." We don't know what Google calls them. Gadgets probably. Anyway. Click the *Twitter* one. It will grab the title of your blog (so make it catchy or at least interesting) and the URL to that post and take you to Twitter. Sign in and the Tweet is sent! How many hundreds if not more than a thousand people just got your tweet? They could be at work, sitting in the airport somewhere, suddenly they get a tweet that is interesting to them. Like say, maybe because the title is about their pain or community involvement? Yes! So they merely tap their device and like magic they are taken to your blog. They read it and like it, they see the blog archive, your links to LinkedIn and Facebook, they can go view your online portfolio!

How and when else can you have the opportunity to share this quality and quantity of information and your expertise in front of even one person, let alone so many? Probably not even in an interview can you do all that! And you have just done it with scores of key players in your industry! Now do the same with G+, Circles, Facebook and LinkedIn! Now you are looking at hitting a Grand Slam! The icing on the cake here is this: all these people can re-tweet and share it via Twitter, Google+ and Facebook.

You need to add just one more piece to the sharing puzzle here. Share a brief snippet from each post on your LinkedIn site, and be sure you include the link so your followers can check out the entire post if they wish. The snippet will serve as a teaser that may cause a recruiter or hiring manager to learn a little more about you. Babe Ruth will have nothing on you!

To do your LinkedIn post, go to your home page (not your profile page), and just underneath your name is the link called *Publish a Post*. Once you click on that, put in the headline (the same as your blog post title), copy and paste the thesis from your post and then follow it with the link to your blog post. Feel free to add photos, videos, tweets, the whole nine yards. LinkedIn refers to this media as "rich media." It has kind of a nice ring to it. And when you score your job, the term "rich media" will have a whole new meaning!

When you publish your LinkedIn post, a notification will automatically be sent to your connections. The idea is they like what they will see and what they see is you. So be sure you are writing about what is important to the employers. Address their pain points and community involvement.

Web Pages

Creating a web page can be as fun as it is valuable. There are several free ones and a seemingly infinite number you can pay for. Our suggestion is to look at the free ones first and see if they will fit your needs and do justice to your product. Who is it that needs a website? Not everybody, to be perfectly frank. If you have products to show, which will either not fit onto or get their just due on your blog, Facebook or LinkedIn, you need a website of some sort. Among these will be graphic designers, architects, web masters, manufacturing professionals and probably anyone who can see or touch the product. Even Lance's scuba experiment had a link to the photo-sharing site Shutterfly. As it turned out, it had great value. It was easy to locate and viewing the pictures was a snap. Students were able to post their photos and were able to order prints and an array of photo gifts from the entire site. Oh yes – videos as well. He even included a calendar, and a journal for them to participate in. If you can show customers interacting in a positive way with your product, you have a very powerful media force working for you.

Contrast that to Pinterest or Instagram. On these sites you can create albums, follow others and be followed by others, but as far as we can discover, there is not any way to order photos. This may be an advantage to you in protecting intellectual properties.

There are many more website builders, which are not so image-intensive and give a more traditional web experience. The best part is, you do not need to know HTML or write one character of code! We'd be lost if that was a requirement to create a website. Some of the more well-known website builders include Wix, Weebly, Yola and WordPress, but there are many more. Just go to your favorite search engine and look for some. Select two or three that appear to fit the bill, and start building them out. You will know right way, which one will work and those that will not. Our experience with them is they are fast, easy and fun to do. Lance has done websites for travel, family and for teaching professionals "how to" in a classroom setting. His favorite is when he has a skeptical client in class, insisting it would be too difficult to do. So he takes five or ten minutes to build one out right then and there. He can even start customizing it for the client. However, he never gives it to him! He is glad to show the way, but the more you can do on your own, the more powerful and self-reliant you become. You do not want to be at anyone's mercy! We have always found the strongest team members are the ones who need the least and contribute the most.

Whatever you do, make your LinkedIn URL evident and include your web URL on your blog and LinkedIn page at a minimum. You may even want to hyperlink your website on the top of your resume as you did your LinkedIn URL. Every time you update your web, blast a message out via LinkedIn, Twitter and G+ Circles. Remember, the more traffic you get on all the sites the higher you will come up in searches.

The name of your website should reflect your profession and somehow identify you. For example, Lance's was *Farr Better Scuba Instruction*. But this name is too long for the top of a resume. So he might just use a single word or short phrase in the place of it. Perhaps: *Website* or *Portfolio*. Make it obvious and simple, there is not a need to be extravagant.

Showcase Your Expertise checklist

_____ I can create my own blog – there are plenty of free blogsites available, including Google Blogger.

_____ Creating my blog isn't enough – I have to share it with my network.

_____ Websites are a great way to share my expertise as well. There are a number of sites that will allow me to create my own website – and I don't have to be a programmer!

_____ Be sure and include my LinkedIn URL on my blog and my website.

_____ Include the URL for my blog on my website, and the URL for my website on my blog.

_____ Contact all my LinkedIn, Twitter and G+ Circles connections and tweeple whenever I update my blog or website.

E-mail

In some (most) social media circles, e-mail is not considered as social media, but we think it is at least in the same genus and shares a few DNA strands with "official" social media that we decided to share a bit about it here. And besides, it represents such an important tool in your job-search quiver that we just didn't feel right leaving it out of this book.

When it comes to using e-mail as a tool in your job search, here's what we recommend:

Identify all your friends and acquaintances who might be in a position to know of jobs that might be available. Let them know you are looking for a job, and what your skills and experience are. A few years' ago when Dan had been laid off, he scoured his e-mail, LinkedIn and Facebook pages for individuals to include in an e-mail list. His initial group totaled over 400 individuals – friends, neighbors, former work acquaintances (including a number at his former firm), fellow church members, vendors who had called on him, etc. Dan developed an e-mail list with all their e-mail addresses, then sent them the following e-mail:

Subject: A little assistance please!

Greetings,

As some of you on this list may know, the law firm I have been at for the past decade has decided to outsource my role, so I am actively seeking a position at another firm or company. You are receiving this e-mail because you are someone I know and trust, and I am hoping you will assist me. As you know, most positions in today's work environment are gotten through networking. It occurred to me that all of you know far more people and have many more contacts in companies than I could ever possibly have, and that's where I need your assistance.

Periodically, I will send you a list of companies to which I have applied. Applying to companies today is generally through a faceless website, which then scrubs your resume for key words. If you have the right key words, and the right number of them, your resume is forwarded to the hiring manager. If you do not have the specific key words, even though you may be the best qualified applicant, your resume may never be forwarded to a hiring manager.

And that's where you come in. If you know someone at one of the companies at which I have applied, a kind word to your contact on my behalf might enable my resume to reach them – or they might be willing to call my resume to the attention of the hiring manager. Or – even though they have my resume, it may be in a stack of 100s of resumes. Your kind word might be just the motivation for the hiring manager to seek and review my resume, especially if you attach my resume for them to review (I have attached my resume for your review and forwarding if you feel it appropriate).

I promise future e-mails will be much shorter, consisting mainly of the list of companies to which I have recently applied.

While you have my resume, let me share a few highlights:

– I am seeking a senior HR position (Director or VP)

– I have 20 years of progressively more responsible HR experience

– I have an MBA

– I am SPHR certified (sort of like a CPA designation for accountants)

81

If you have questions, please ask away. You may contact me at wdanielquillen@gmail.com or 303-555-1212.

Thanks for your assistance and consideration!

Daniel Quillen

Responses were immediate from many of those to whom I sent the e-mail. I received many well wishes, and more than a few job leads from that initial e-mail. What's more, I now had over 400 people (my LinkedIn network and other friends and acquaintances) out in the business world, keeping their eyes and ears open for positions that might be appropriate for me.

Much of your job search will also center around e-mail.

Don't forget the power and utility of e-mail.

Your network can be one of your most powerful allies during your job hunt – so don't abandon them! You began your job hunt by sharing an e-mail with your network, informing them of your new status – part of the army of the unemployed. As your job hunt progresses, be sure to continue to include them in your search. Your follow-up e-mails shouldn't be as lengthy as the first one, but they should still contain information and requests that may help you end your unemployment. Here's an e-mail Dan sent as he neared the end of his job search (but of course he didn't know that at the time!):

Hello All,

Still looking. Had a few good interviews last week, and a few scheduled for this week. Below are the companies where I have applied over the past two weeks. As before, if you know someone at any of these companies, I'd appreciate knowing.

Dan Q.

Interviews:
eBay (Salt Lake City)

Intrawest (Alisha Smith and Margot Jones)
Newmont Mining (Sheri Brown)
Sundyne (Hamilton SunStrand) (Angela Thomson)

(Author's note: the names of the managers with whom Dan interviewed were changed to protect the innocent!)

Baker & McKenzie (Chicago)
Children's Hospital
Comcast
Comex Group
DCP Mainstream LLC
Dish Network
Hitachi
Petroleum Development Corp.
Steven Roberts Originals
Trimble
Volvo Rents
Webroot

By the way, it was interesting to go back in his e-mail archives and find an example of one of these my-job-search-is-still-continuing e-mails Dan had sent. There are sixteen companies in the list above, and he ended up interviewing with four of them – a 25% hit rate, which was pretty consistent throughout his time of unemployment.

We will note here that even though Dan was sending these e-mails to hundreds of individuals – his network – not all of them responded to each e-mail, so don't expect that to be the case when you send e-mails similar to this. Typically, however, he would hear from between 15% and 25% of his network – some had contacts at his targeted companies, or who knew someone at one of the companies, or even the hiring manager. Many would send a response something along the lines of:

Dan,

Sorry to hear you haven't found something yet, but looks like you are working hard. I don't know any of these people or have contacts at any of these companies, but I will keep you in my thoughts, and hope positive things come your way real soon!

Angie

Don't be discouraged because every e-mail you send doesn't get a response from everyone in your network. But you are keeping your situation – unemployed and looking for work! – in front of them, whether they take the time to read your e-mail or not! We like to think every member of his network read and considered all his e-mails, but realistically we doubt it. But we know that once a week or so, hundreds of people were reminded that Dan was looking for work.

Finally, once your job hunt is successful – and it will be! – don't forget those who helped you get there. The day Dan accepted a job, he sent the following e-mail to his network of friends, those who had helped during his job hunt:

All,

This morning my job hunt came to a successful conclusion – I accepted an offer to be the Division Manager of Human Resources at the City of Aurora. I start mid-week next week. I will be doing essentially the same job I did for ten years at HRO, but for 3,500 employees rather than HRO's 500.

Thank you so much for your support and assistance, whether it was reaching out to individuals you knew to put in a good word for me, letting me know about jobs you had run across, wishing me well through e-mail or in person, and your positive thoughts and/or prayers in my behalf. It really did make a difference and helped me stay focused and encouraged.

Thanks again for your support!

Dan Quillen

E-mail is a quick and effective way of reaching out to your network of friends and colleagues. In fact, a recruiter friend of ours feels so strongly about how effective networking can be that he tells his candidates: "Your network is your net worth."

And finally – one last tidbit of e-mail advice: be certain you check your e-mail frequently – at least daily, preferably several times throughout the day. Recently, at Dan's current employer, we were filling the position of a benefits administrator. We screened the resumes and identified five individuals we wanted to interview. On a Monday afternoon Dan sent e-mails to the top five candidates, inviting them in for an interview three days hence – on Thursday. Most of the candidates responded within hours of the request. As the day of the interviews approached, he still hadn't heard from one of the candidates. Dan reached out again on Wednesday afternoon and offered him an interview slot on either Thursday or Friday. He never responded.

We went forward with our interviews. The last candidate we interviewed was exceptional, so we offered her the position on Thursday afternoon.

On Friday afternoon, the candidate who hadn't responded e-mailed to say he had been away from his e-mail for a few days and would love to interview with us. Dan had to tell him that he was sorry, but the position had already been offered to another candidate. Don't miss out on interviews because you don't check your e-mail frequently!

People are busier in the American workplace than they have ever been. Sometimes hiring managers will try to bring candidates in between several meetings or projects that are due, and sometimes short notice of interview opportunities is given. Dan has e-mailed candidates hoping they would be available the next day for an interview. If you only check your e-mail once a day, or several times a week, you may very well miss out on a golden opportunity! Note: Dan cuts candidates slack if they are not available the next day!

As you can see, e-mail isn't nearly as svelte nor robust as many of the other social media options, but it still has its place in your job search arsenal!

E-mail checklist
_____ Don't forget about using the capabilities of e-mail to reach out to my network.

_____ I should create an e-mail list of all my friends, former co-workers, neighbors, etc.

_____ I should send my e-mail list information about my job search – companies I am interested in, interviewing with, etc.

_____ When I am seeking a new position, let all my network know.

_____ Check my e-mail frequently so I don't miss offers for interviews with short turn-around times.

_____ Don't forget to thank my network once I find my new job!

Getting Company Information

Now that you have your social media sites up and running, we will teach you some more ways to get very valuable contact and information you can leverage during your job-search process.

Reference USA

Reference USA is a premier source of business information that is well designed to be easily data mined. Currently there is information on over 43 million businesses in the USA alone. There is also information on nearly two million Canadian companies.

To access it Lance traveled down to his local library and asked for the Reference Librarian. He was able to set up his account with Reference USA in less than five minutes and the price of admission was not exorbitant – it merely required his library card. And since he already had the card he did not incur any additional fees. Now Lance can access the database from anywhere with an internet connection.

After logging into Reference USA and choosing one of the ten available databases, you will find a *Quick Search* and an *Advanced Search*. The *Quick Search* is good if you know either the name of a company or an Executive's first and last name. The *Advanced Search* is the one we use almost every time. So let's take a look at it, shall we?

On the left portion of the screen, you will find a couple of dozen headings divided into about ten groups. These are all filters to narrow down the millions of companies in the database.

For our example, we'll say you are a finance executive with years of experience in brokerage, living in the Denver Metro Area. We will choose:

- Business Type

    – Major Industry Group

- Geography

    – Metro Area

- Number of Employees

Now we will get the resulting filters of this search:

- Major Industry

    – Finance, Insurance & Real Estate

        – Security and Commodities Brokerage

            – Security Brokerage & Dealers

- State: Colorado

- Metro Area (they currently list 17 for Colorado): Denver-Aurora-Lakewood

- Number of Employees (currently there are nine ranges to choose from): 1000-4999

Off to the right you have the option of choosing *View Results* or *Update Count*. Experience has taught us to *Update Count* first. Sometimes the number of results can be overwhelming. If that happens, simply select more filters and *Update Count*. So let's see what happens here: there are 963. That is a lot of businesses to sift through. Therefore, add a couple of more filters underneath the last one. Choose two more: *Stock & Bond Brokers* and *Mutual Funds*. Now click *Update Count* again. This time you only get 189, of which 158 are Stock & Bond Brokers and 48 Mutual Funds. Altogether, this took less than two minutes to do.

Now you are ready to *View Results*. They display 25 at a time. You will notice there are multiple branches for the same brokerage. However, almost all are recognizable names to us. In the right column is an indicator for the corporate tree. As we are not interested in the local branch right now, choose the tree.

You can now view the eight major divisions of the company. The Group Inc., LLCs, Holding Company, and The Investment Advisor. We see there are about 2,000 total employees and sales volume of over $953 billion. We will choose the Group Inc.

Here is where the fun begins! You can see the phone number to the main office and the mailing address! What can we do with these? Just wait! We're gonna show ya!

Next there are some job listings, but these may not be all of them.

The next item is the Industry Profile with SIC and NACIS codes. Therefore, if your interest is in one or more of the corresponding descriptions, you can write these codes down and search companies using SIC and NACIS codes in the *Advanced Search* area.

There are several more areas of interesting and useful information. However, we want to bring your attention to the two golden nuggets – the real reason we brought you down this path.

First is the *Management Directory*. This institution is showing twenty-nine executives, by name, title, gender and ethnicity! And guess what? We have their addresses! So what are we going to do with that information? Resume and cover letter time. (Connect with as many of them on LinkedIn as you can. Do not set your expectations too high however; our experience has taught us that the players in this sandbox are not commonly found. But when you do, it can be very worthwhile!)

Find the person in the management directory you are most likely to have in your reporting chain. Do your homework (see the next chapter on

Homework). Tailor a cover letter and resume, print them on good white, bond paper, use a matching envelope and mail it regular mail. Yes, regular mail. In fact, use your best handwriting to address the envelope. It looks personal enough to slip past lots of gatekeepers. If you use overnight, or make it look official, count on it being opened by the gatekeeper and never making it to your executive.

Does this really work? Yes, that is why we are telling you to do it. Here's a real-life example:

Lance was working with a fixed income trader, who had been trading directly on the Street for a boutique firm and prior to that for one of the big three brokerages. Lance asked him where he would like to work. He named a $52 billion company with 185,000 employees that we all know and love. He had analyzed their issued debt many times and was impressed with the cash flow the company has. He felt he could really contribute to their bottom line in the treasury management department. OK.

So they looked the company up on Reference USA, found the CFO, did their homework and wrote her a cover letter and resume specifically outlining how Lance's job seeker could contribute to making money on their cash. They printed it on good resume paper, stuffed it neatly into a matching envelope, hand addressed it and mailed it with a regular stamp.

About one week later, Lance's job seeker received a call from the head of Human Resources requesting an interview! What must have happened was that the CFO read and was sufficiently impressed by the cover letter, hyperlinked resume and online profiles, to walk down the hall to the head of Human Resources and have a conversation. Now who is going to tell the CFO, "No, I think you are wrong"? Even the hiring manager would much rather go to the CFO and thank her for the lead and what a wonderful and valuable employee he was able to hire thanks to her!

That is why you want to use the management directory.

We told you there was a second golden nugget. This one is dead easy:

Down at the bottom of the *Results* page is a section titled: *Competitors' Report*. That will show about ten competitors of the company you are researching.

Therefore, if you might like to work for the company you looked up, maybe any or all of these ten would fit the bill as well! 1 = 10! Who knew?

Another targeted source of job listings

I want to show you a little-known way to get great results for specific job postings right on company web pages. Beat all the job aggregators and job boards and do not miss these jobs, many of which may be posted only to the company's career page. Recruiters do not always post jobs on public boards, however, because of common Human Resource requirements; many companies will post all or nearly all open job announcements on the company page.

All you need to know is a little **Google-fu** (sort of like Kung-Fu…). Syntax in the URL must be exact here. When you upload a resume and cover letter during the job application process there is a very good chance it will be scanned by an electronic "reader." The reader will be looking for key words and phrases (most if not all of which are found on the job posting you are responding to). You already know how to leverage that for your benefit. However, did you know you can have Google and other search engines search specifically for company career pages using these readers? In addition, for *your* job and your geographic location? It is easy.

One of the most popular reading apps is the Oracle product Taleo, which seems to be the industry standard. There are others such as Talent Cloud, G2Crowd, KNXA, iCiMS and others. All we have to do is tell our favorite search engine how to search for jobs we're interested in with companies using these products! And here is how you do it!

Remember – careful with the syntax on this maneuver – In the URL line, to begin with, type the following:

site:taleo.net intitle:careers

Then, add your job title and any filter words you may want to use. We can look at a real-life example:

site:taleo.net intitle:careers engineer

Find hidden jobs: learn how to use Google-fu!

This little snippet in the URL line yielded about 5,730 postings in 0.45 seconds on Google! All of which were actively on company careers pages at that moment! Take that, nasty job boards!

To narrow your search to the type of engineering job you are looking for, add a descriptor word following what you just searched with. I added aircraft:

site:taleo.net intitle:careers engineer aircraft

This filter word fine-tuned my results to 269 results. Note: there must be a space between the follow-on words (see above).

If you are targeting a geographic area, add it in:

site:taleo.net intitle:careers aircraft Denver

This brought our results down to seven. Do not forget, not all employers call the same job by the same name. We switched "aircraft" for "aeronautical" and found nine jobs in the Denver area. That is a targeted job search for currently open positions!

Use the same syntax to find other career opportunities using any of the other reading apps out there. For example:

site: G2Crowd.com intitle:careers human resources

(Note: When using Google-fu, be sure and use the .net, .com, etc. suffix to the company name in your Google-fu string.)

Now you can go to work on LinkedIn, Reference USA, Twitter and Facebook finding networking contacts, understanding the employer, tweaking your profiles as needed and preparing a targeted resume and cover letter. Make the application, upload your targeted resume and let the reading app go to work for you! As you score enough hits on key words and phrases your cover letter and resume will come before human eyes! When those eyes behold your customized resume using word recognition, the owner of those eyes will want to read it in detail. He or she will see the hyperlink to your LinkedIn and blog or web pages, control click on the links and we got 'em right where we want 'em, just like a Venus Fly Trap!

This is so much better than mindlessly filling out application after application! Recently Lance worked with an over-40 job seeker who was an operations manager in a manufacturing company in Denver. If you are not aware, Denver is not known to be a manufacturing hub – making these jobs hard to find. Before coming into Lance's office, he had put out over 100 resumes and applications. His results? One phone call from a recruiter. That was it. The poor man was feeling really bad about himself. He and Lance sat down and went to work getting him up to speed on today's job seeking skills. One day is all they spent on this. Over the next week he applied for ten jobs; he received eight interviews and two job offers!

That is the power that change can bring. Are you ready to make that change?

Getting Company Information checklist

_____ Reference USA is a great place to find out information about companies and individuals with whom I am interviewing.

_____ Use the Competitors' Report to find companies similar to those in which I am interested.

_____ Learn about Google-fu, and use it!

_____ Many of the jobs I find using Google-fu are only located on company websites – not on job boards.

_____ Am I ready for the changes social media can bring to my job search?

Homework

No, this is not an assignment to do thirty story problems or write a 1,500 word essay comparing and contrasting Steinbeck with Melville. Thankfully that brain damage is done.

This is more like intelligence gathering. Like James Bond or the Black Widow!

Company Pages

Most all companies today have a web page, Facebook, LinkedIn, Twitter, YouTube and usually one or two more like Pinterest or Instagram and others. By going to the company website, you can easily find out which ones they are using. Each one will have value to you in creating your social media presence and positioning yourself for the written resume and interview. We will start with the company pages. We like shopping at the outdoor clothing and goods store REI so let's start there. Continually ask yourself two questions while viewing the pages:

1. What is the message they are sending, and

2. How does that apply to me as a job seeker?

On the home page of REI it seems first about savings and second about product. So value would be a major message. At the bottom, there is a common link, which you must check out for every company to which you apply: *About Us.* (The wording may be a little different from company to company. REI's, for example, is *Who we are.*) By following the link, we learn "100% customer satisfaction" is a major concern, conservation efforts and company culture are the others. If you are serious about working for REI, your social media profiles and all your communications with REI need to reflect these values. This is a great time to showcase your experience – and more importantly – your contributions to these core values on your blog, Twitter, Facebook and online portfolio. Be sure all the professional connections you are making at REI have the opportunity to enjoy these posts and tweets.

Lest you think this retail example is not applicable to you we assure you it is. What do you think it takes to run a $1,800,000,000 retail company? The jobs we see in the store are not representative of the breadth or scope of this employer. A look at the job page tells a better story. The job functions listed there include carpentry, administration, accounting, IT, e-commerce, public affairs, legal, marketing, facilities and others. No matter what your field, you must tell the same story in order to "fit in." If Dan was promoting fracking, hunting and land development on his social media sites, he might not be viewed as the right person for REI. However, he might be the right person for Cabela's, Bass Pro Shops or Encana. In other words, you need to be sending the same message the employer is and certainly not a contrary one.

And by the way – if you really are a hunter, believe in fracking and land development, you may not be happy at a company whose corporate culture is opposed to those activities.

Another great page on company websites is the *Investor* or *Investor Relations* page. REI is not a publicly traded company, so we do not expect to find such a page on their site (and we didn't). Let's try the pharmaceutical firm Merck.

Right at the top of Merck's home page is a link for *Investors*. Why do we care about the investors' page? Go look at it with us and you will see a gold mine, not even a nugget, but an entire gold mine of what is going on and where the company is heading! Talk about being able to position yourself as a valuable future employee, here it is!

There are links to their *Product Pipeline* (sales people, chemical engineers and biologists pay attention to this one). *Mergers and Spin Offs* (MBAs and attorneys here), *Financial Reports* (everyone!) What? Everyone. Yep. Not only the usual suspects here, but also everyone. You do not need to know how to read a company balance sheet to find value on the Financial reports page. What we are after for the whole family is the *Annual Report*. It happens to be a PDF for Merck, so open it up. Do two things with it: first, browse the subjects and see if any apply to you. For example, there is a discussion on an increasing dependency on sophisticated information technology and infrastructure. IT professionals and project managers, we hope you see some pain points you can address.

Now for everybody: find the message from the CEO. Sometimes it is the first thing and other times it takes a little searching for, as with this one. On Merck's website it is under *Management's Discussion and Analysis of Financial Condition and Results of Operations*. Yes, it does not sound as fun as going to the movies on Friday night, but the information you gather will not only help you "look like the job" on social media, but it will help you in the interview process. Imagine being able to have a conversation with the hiring manager about where the company is heading, how his or her department is contributing to it and…drum roll here…imagine the impact of you giving specific examples of how you contributed to past employers involved with the same or similar directions! Like we said at the beginning of this book: *"…be brave, go into waters in which you have not ventured. Knowledge is power. Power to change, power to influence, power to grow."*

Company websites, investor and financial pages in particular, have a wealth of information valuable to me!

You will find a plethora of other good sources of powerful information on the company website, so do yourself a favor and put a little effort into your homework!

Like any good instructor, we are going to review some of the critical elements we've learned to this point:

LinkedIn: The Backbone of your job search

LinkedIn is not just the foundation of what we have learned, but also the very backbone of all our efforts. It is the space of recruiters, job postings and networking. More likely than not, this is where your recruiter will find you.

Blogs

Blogging, online portfolios and websites are the showcases of your industry expertise. There is not anywhere else you can put forth your skills and experiences so vividly and in such detail. Not even in an interview.

Twitter

Twitter is the notification system. Twitter is the oil which makes the social media engine run smoothly. Do not forget, it is also a valuable resource for jobs, networking and homework.

Facebook

Facebook provides a peek into who you really are. You are like your Facebook friends and posts. Remember – your Facebook pages need to be Puritan clean here. Facebook, like Twitter, is also a good source for jobs, networking and homework.

Homework checklist

_____ I can learn a LOT about companies from their websites.

_____ Information I learn from company websites will help me learn what the company's pain points are.

_____ By carefully reviewing the websites of companies I am interested in, I can make sure I look like them – have the same interests and drives.

_____ Be true to myself – if a company I am learning about has values or priorities that do not agree with my core values and beliefs, I should look elsewhere.

_____ Check out the Investor pages of the company's website – great information may be available there.

Resumes

Resumes continue to be a valuable element in the job hunt process for the job seeker, recruiter, hiring manager and networking. Most application processes will ask for a resume to be uploaded. Therefore, it is a tool the uses of which we need to understand and leverage to our benefit.

First of all, understanding how HR experts use it feels like a good place to start.

It will be looked at one or two times during an evaluation phase by Human Resources. Notice we did not say "it will be read one or two times..." If a resume is tailored properly (more on that is upcoming) your resume will be seen by human eyes. Ask yourself a question here: How long do you think it will be looked at on average during the first round? A minute, three minutes, thirty seconds?

Try five seconds.

We know Human Resource recruiters who say they *never* spend more than three seconds on the first look! That sounds more like a quick glance, doesn't it? The challenge this creates for you is easy to understand, and not all that hard to accomplish. Yet very few job seekers really do. The challenge: does your resume clearly communicate enough of the proper information in three to five seconds to warrant being put into the review-later stack?

The test is simple. If for every ten applications and resumes you send out, are you getting three to five interview offers? If so, pass jail and land on go! If not, read on and open your mind. We say this because of the sheer number of job seekers we have worked with who have paid good money (sometimes well over a thousand dollars) to have their resumes profession-ally crafted, and yet they do not get more than one interview for every twenty resumes and applications! We know people who have sent out over 100 without a single employer interview! We really hope this does not de-scribe the boat you are in. But if it is, all the more reason to pay attention.

The next step for the Human Resource recruiter is actually reading your resume in detail. Those who have tailored a resume correctly will be con-sidered for an interview. That is where we want you to be.

Remember, not all resumes and applications submitted will get looked at by a human recruiter or hiring manager, no matter what the qualifica-tions of the applicant are. It is really a matter of practicality on the part of the interviewing and hiring authority. If 200 applicants have successfully submitted their applications online, the automated resume reader searches and prioritizes all 200 resumes based on the amount of "hits" on key words and phrases each resume receives. Some of those resumes – the ones that don't have the requisite number of hits on key words – won't make it to a human to review.

Don't believe us? Here is a concrete example of something that happened to Dan; he shared it in *The Perfect Resume* and some of his other books as well. Shortly after Dan had been laid off, he was up late (actually early) in the wee hours of the morning, searching for opportunities. He came across a job ad he had seen before, and had decided he wasn't interested. This time, however, he thought, "Why not?" and decided to apply. He printed off the job ad, highlighted the key words and experience they were seeking, and tailored his resume for the position. Dan knew he wasn't a perfect fit for the job, but still had many of the skills and experiences they were seek-ing. At 2:46am he submitted his application.

Immediately – at 2:46am – he received an e-mail in his Inbox from that company, acknowledging his submission. Among other things, they told him:

> Your background, skills and experience will be reviewed against the position you have selected.

At 2:56am – exactly ten minutes later – Dan received a rejection e-mail, which included the following:

> Your background and qualifications have been given careful review with respect to this position. Although you were not selected for this position we appreciate your desire to expand your career.

We know HR departments are overworked and work long hours, but we are certain it wasn't an HR person who gave Dan's resume a "careful review" between 2:46am and 2:56am on that Monday morning in July! As we mentioned, his experience was not a perfect fit for the job, and the applications software obviously thought so as well. In its review of his resume, it did not see a key word or key words it was looking for, and the result was his rejection as a candidate.

Okay – so let's say you believe us and you have tailored your resume so that the applications software sees enough key words to send your resume to a human. The human recruiter will then start a five-second review process until he or she finds, typically, ten resumes to review in depth later. Then the in-depth reading takes place, which means one to two minutes per resume at the longest. One to two minutes tells us the resume must be easily read and communicate the needed skills and experiences very precisely. The group of ten will then be pared down to three or four! What happens if you were number eleven? Never even looked at, even if you were the most qualified! Do you like it? No. Is it fair? Probably so. After all, the company is not necessarily trying to hire "the best" there is, but rather, an employee who can do the job well.

Make sure my resume uses the appropriate key words.

Here is a bit of HR mindset for you that will help you get your mind around it all. The first look is to determine who NOT to interview, the in-depth read is to determine who TO interview. Go figure. For you, the resume only has one purpose…any guesses? Right! To get an interview. The entire package from social media to interview follow up gets you the job offer.

Before we discuss each of the sections of a good resume, let's mention a few sections that you should *not* include in your resume.

Objective sections. We're not big fans of *Objective* sections, and if we receive a resume with them, we typically just ignore them. Unless someone has forgotten to change their objective and it says something like:

> Seeking to use my experience and skills in a management position in the healthcare industry.

That's all fine and good, except the position we have open is not in the healthcare industry! If we run across a resume with an *Objective* section like that, there are already 2.5 strikes against that candidate. We don't reject it outright, but close.

Personal sections. Again, we are not fans of these sections. We may sound like resume curmudgeons, so no offense, but we have absolutely zero interest in your hobbies, marital status, volunteer work or other such personal tidbits. You were a Division 1A collegiate or professional athlete? We'll admit that's impressive. But we prefer to see information like that in an *Awards/Honors* section, or in your cover letter.

Not long ago, we reviewed a professional resume with the following *Personal* section:

> Married to Cindy, a ceramic artist and potter. We have two sons, Scott, a biologist and Anthony, a music teacher. My family and I enjoy swimming, biking, hiking, skiing, camping, climbing mountains, golf and most any outdoor activities. We also enjoy cultural experiences including art, music, and travel.

Now we are certain Cindy is a lovely woman, and Scott and Anthony are perfectly delightful children, but none of that is something we have the slightest bit of interest in as hiring managers. (Note: names in the above paragraph have been changed…!)

The only exception we have run across in our review of tens of thousands of resumes is one candidate's *Personal* section that included the fact that he had led a blind climber up Kilimanjaro and Mt. Everest. Now that is something we found impressive!

References Available Upon Request. We sure wish we had a dollar for every resume we have reviewed with that unnecessary ditty appended at the end of a resume. That is assumed. We have yet to ask a candidate for their references and had them say, "No, I think not."

Okay, now that we have that out of our system, let's get to the resume sections we believe are viable and important to have in your resume.

We have been able to find a successful format and a method to fill the format that is particularly effective. (Obviously, or we would not be telling you about it!) If you've read *The Perfect Resume* or *Get a Job!*, Dan shared the format there. But in case you haven't picked up those critical tomes for any job hunter's personal library, we will show you the format in the next couple of pages. Please do not jump to the format and start writing your resume, until we have discussed the content. You must have both format and content. Otherwise, it is like the recruiter stepping into a beautiful sports car, to find out it is powered by a lawn mower engine! That's a tough sell right there!

For review, we will begin with the top section again, but in more detail. We'll also move through each of the sections we think are effective elements of resumes.

Dr. Richard L. Farr

Denver CO   LinkedIn Blog   303-555-1212   DrFarr@gmail.com

Lance's name stands out nice and bold. This is what recruiters have told us they want to see. Easily identified. We prefer Times New Roman as our resume font and 24 point size for your name. We use single spacing between the name and contact information.

There is a school of thought out there now that feels including your home address on your resume is not necessary, and in fact, may be used against you. When Dan was director of Human Resources at a large law firm, Dan was helping one of our partners review resumes. We came to one candidate

Dan thought was pretty strong. But the partner dismissed her instantly. She said, "She lives an hour from our office – she'll never want to make that drive."

Rather than include your address, use the space to include links to your LinkedIn profile and in this case your blog (or online portfolio). Also, you can see above Lance's cell phone number and e-mail: of course, they are not really his! Nor is it his resume. We're not even sure what most of the statements mean. But we do understand the format of each! The point size here should be 11 or 12 and the line is a 3-point line. If you are using Word, use the draw function to draw the line – in our experience, that works the best.

The following section is the *Summary*. Notice it is not an *Objective* statement. Your objective is to get a job! Don't forget that, EVER!

Summary

An Industrial Engineer (IE) who thrives in a dynamic and challenging manufacturing environment. Proven track record of results using cutting-edge systems and processes toward exceeding expectations in Return on Investment, Delivery, Quality, and Cost Reduction.

The word *Summary* is bold, Times New Roman, 14 point and obviously underlined. The content of the summary is 11 or 12 point. It is based on – you guessed it – the job posting you are applying to. Not four or six other jobs, but The Job, That Job. It is important to point out, the summary addressed the characteristics of "who" the employer is looking for, not so much what the employee is looking for. You want the employer to make the subtle connection "this is who we are looking for." So carefully read the entire job posting and write down the traits and characteristics of the employee the employer is seeking. Each point in the summary MUST (no fudging) address the job posting.

The next part is a little tricky to format if you are not too familiar with Word. It is going to be nine bullet points in three columns of three, each one on just one line. (We'll explain our madness here momentarily.) Following are a few pointers on how you do it.

Glean the job posting for the nine most important skills (the "what's") that you can best address and prove. Next type all nine in one descending column, highlight the column and click on the bullet function:

- Manager
- Project Manager
- Outsourcing
- Interpersonal Skills
- Mentor
- Process Improvement
- Problem Solver
- Capacity Planner
- Six Sigma

With the column still highlighted, go under Layout and choose Columns, Three. Set the section off with double spaces above and below:

• Manager	• Project Manager	• Outsourcing
• Interpersonal Skills	• Process Improvement	• Mentor
• Problem Solver	• Capacity Planner	• Six Sigma

The result is the nine most important keywords that will stand out to the automated resume reader and the human resource recruiter. Remember, the recruiter is not at all likely to be a subject matter expert in your field, so he or she will use word recognition from the same job posting you read. In fact, they may well have written it! Guess what? Because we read three to five words at a time, left to right top to bottom and use word recognition to do it, it will take the human resource professional less than three seconds to see that you have what they are looking for at first glance! Welcome to the *resume-review-in-depth* crowd!

The next section is the so-called work history. How boring is that for a title on a resume? In place of boredom, step it up a notch. We will call it *Professional Experience.*

Professional Experience
In this section, you will put the title of each job, with a descriptor if called for. For example: **Team Lead/Project Management**. Bold and underlined.

Place the company name and your years of tenure there underneath you name, with the years justified right (years are fine here).

Single space to your well-crafted three to five achievement statements, each one preceded by a bullet point. Let's see how that looks:

Industrial Engineering Supervisor

Boeing, Everett, WA   2003-2004

- Managed the redesign of a manufacturing shop floor using CAD, which increased workflow by 25%, and reduced work-related accidents by 47%.
- Managed a cross-functional team (IE, Planning, Engineering, Quality Assurance, Manufacturing, Tooling, etc.) which implemented Lean Manufacturing and Six Sigma to enhance production.
- Managed the implementation of a Kanban system which improved workflow by 35%.
- Received three Outstanding Achievement Awards and Recognitions, including one presented by the Vice President over Manufacturing Operations.

Lead Industrial Engineer

Boeing, Everett, WA   1999-2003

- Saved the company over $10 Million in costly tooling through effective capacity and resource planning.
- Developed from scratch a Standards and Tool Crib (significantly under budget and ahead of schedule), increasing overall parts/tool acquisition efficiency by 300%.
- Led Material Requirements Planning (MRP) implementation as the site key user; tested the new software, designed curriculum, and organized, scheduled and implemented training of 40 IEs toward an unprecedented and seamless (no downtime) and on-time implementation.
- Successfully led and trained eleven Industrial Engineers, assessing skills and assigning to appropriate responsibilities.
- Received five Outstanding Achievement Awards and Recognitions.

Industrial Engineer (Outsourcing)

Boeing, Everett, WA   1995-1997

- Negotiated contracts with Boeing subsidiaries and outside suppliers toward outsourcing assembly work, successfully creating core competencies.
- Transferred all responsibility for the 767 forward landing gear to BF Goodrich, including complete analysis of a 4,000-part bill of material, resulting in 100% on-time delivery of first unit.
- Conducted a precedent-setting work transfer of 200 minor subassemblies to a sheltered workshop to train the disabled, which set the standard for many successful follow-on transfers.

There are a few things to point out here. Double spacing between sections only, three to five short and easily-read achievement statements to each section. Never more than two or three lines. Quantify each result whenever possible. Look at the first one mentioned in the resume with us.

- Managed the redesign of a manufacturing shop floor using CAD, (*the situation followed now by the result*) which increased workflow by 25%, and reduced work related-accidents by 47%.

The result can come first:

- Increased workflow by 25%, and reduced work related accidents by 47%, by the proper redesign of a manufacturing shop floor using CAD.

Both will cause the Human Resource professional and the hiring manager to jump for joy and ask you the question: "How did you do that?" So be prepared!

Next will come the *Education* section. A few words here. If you graduated from an Ivy League or similar top-ranked school put the name of the college on top and the degree on the bottom. If not, put the degree on the top and the school on the bottom.

Education
Bachelor's Degree, Industrial Engineering

Purdue University, Summa Cum Laude

Education
Harvard

MBA

Notice what is missing – the year of graduation. If it has been five years or longer since you graduated, leave that informational tidbit off your resume. And you'll also note the GPA has not been included. Our poor Harvard boy barely graduated. But Prude did exceptionally well.

Other sections can be added such as: *Publications, Professional Organizations, Computer Languages & Platforms*, etc.

Here is an example of a finished resume:

Dr. Richard L. Farr

Denver CO   LinkedIn Blog   303-555-1212   DrFarr@gmail.com

Summary

An Industrial Engineer (IE) who thrives in a dynamic and challenging manufacturing environment. Proven track record of results using cutting-edge systems and processes toward exceeding expectations in Return on Investment, Delivery, Quality, and Cost Reduction.

- Manager
- Mentor
- Good Guy
- Project Manager
- Interpersonal Skills
- Capacity Planner
- Outsourcing
- Process Improvement
- Problem Solver

Professional Experience

Industrial Engineering Supervisor

Boeing, Everett, WA   2003-2004

- Managed the redesign of a manufacturing shop floor using CAD, which increased workflow by 25%, and reduced work-related accidents by 47%.

• Managed a cross-functional team (IE, Planning, Engineering, Quality Assurance, Manufacturing, Tooling, etc.) which implemented Lean Manufacturing and Six Sigma to enhance production.
• Managed the implementation of a Kanban system which improved workflow by 35%.
• Received three Outstanding Achievement Awards and Recognitions, including one presented by the Vice President over Manufacturing Operations.

Lead Industrial Engineer

Boeing, Everett, WA   1999-2003

• Saved the company over $10 million in costly tooling through effective capacity and resource planning.
• Developed from scratch a Standards and Tool Crib (significantly under budget and ahead of schedule), increasing overall parts/tool acquisition efficiency by 300%.
• Led Material Requirements Planning (MRP) implementation as the site key user; tested the new software, designed curriculum, and organized, scheduled and implemented training of 40 IEs toward an unprecedented and seamless (no downtime) and on-time implementation.
• Successfully led and trained eleven Industrial Engineers, assessing skills and assigning to appropriate responsibilities.
• Received five Outstanding Achievement Awards and Recognitions.

Industrial Engineer (Outsourcing)

Boeing, Everett, WA   1995-1997

• Negotiated contracts with Boeing subsidiaries and outside suppliers toward outsourcing assembly work, successfully creating core competencies.
• Transferred all responsibility for the 767 forward landing gear to BF Goodrich, including complete analysis of a 4,000-part bill of material, resulting in 100% on-time delivery of first unit.
• Conducted a precedent-setting work transfer of 200 minor subassemblies to a sheltered workshop to train the disabled, which set the standard for many successful follow-on transfers.

• Managed the transfer of all materials for an entire production control area (350,000 part numbers) to a remote site, resulting in 100% on-time delivery and full production under budget and ahead of schedule.
• Received six Outstanding Achievement Awards and Recognitions.

Industrial Engineer (Methods Analysis)

Boeing, Everett, WA   1993-1995

• Developed a low-cost tool, which eliminated a chronic behind-schedule condition on a major sub-assembly. The new tool created 100% schedule recovery within 30 days of installation.
• Led a statistical process-control project, which enabled the implementation of a Just-in-Time system which became the standard for many other implementations throughout the business unit.
• Revamped the tracking process for all parts in the paint shop, which increased parts accountability by over 40%, and reduced rework by 60%.
• Received eleven Outstanding Achievement Awards and Recognitions.

Education

Bachelor's Degree, Industrial Engineering

Purdue University

Professional Training

• Statistical Process Control (120-hour course): Boeing Sponsored
• APICS Certification: Boeing Sponsored
• MRP training (Boeing sponsored): became site key user toward leading site to precedent-setting implementation.

That's it!

Here are some real deal breakers for you to pay very strict attention to:

1. Do not use first person. In fact, don't use any person. Rather than saying "I received eleven outstanding achievement awards and rec-

ognitions." Merely say, "Received eleven outstanding achievement awards and recognitions."

2. No grammatical, punctuation or spelling errors. When Dan was a hiring manager, if he saw one of these errors in a resume he was reviewing, the resume hit the trash can.

3. Only use commonly accepted industry abbreviations.

4. Not more than two pages. Believe it or not, the HR professionals and hiring managers do not want to read a 1,000-plus word document. It also demonstrates good written communications skill to get your message across on two easily read pages. There are a few industries / careers that are notable exceptions to the two-page rule, such as medical, legal, higher education and government jobs. But they are really seeking a curriculum vitae instead of a resume. That is an entire book in and of itself!

With all that said, spell- and grammar-check are very useful. (Lance is very dyslexic, a kind of gift, and lives by the spell-check function.) Better yet, or in addition to, if you know a secondary school English teacher, ask them to proofread it. For example, are you using passive tenses where you should not be or compound past rather that simple past? Do you remember what those are?

Lance had a retired high school English teacher on his staff for some time. She was a great proofreader! Lance thought he was pretty well-versed in grammar and context. She was able to take all of his client and internal documents to a whole new level. She was so happy when Lance gave her an entire box of red pencils to use!

Two final words on resumes. Once your first one is finished save it and use it as a template. That will make your future resumes easier to revise. Also, save the resume to be uploaded as a PDF and submit it in that format. The formatting does not always make it through the upload process intact in other word processing programs.

Resumes checklist
_____ Even though the focus of this book is social media, I still must have a great resume.

_____ My resume must have quantifiable accomplishments throughout.

_____ Absolutely no typos or grammar errors.

_____ My resume should be no more than two pages.

_____ Be careful with abbreviations. If I use them, make sure they are industry-standard abbreviations.

_____ Include the URL for my LinkedIn profile and any relevant blogs or websites I have.

Make sure to pick up Dan's *The Perfect Resume* for much greater detail on how to craft a great resume!

Common Resume Errors

By now, you should have a pretty good feeling about the basics of resume writing – no typos, grammar difficulties, crisp and professional look and feel, good formatting, achievement statements, etc., etc. let us provide a summary of a few things you should keep in mind while you are assembling your resume. Below are the most common resume errors we see often that you should avoid.

Here is the list of Resume forbidden elements:

1. Be honest. We have both reviewed resumes that contradicted themselves between entries or between the resume and the cover letter. Your Summary statement says you have ten years accounting experience? When we add up the experience at your various jobs as listed on your resume, they only come to a little over seven years. Rounding up from seven to ten isn't Kosher. We're always particularly concerned when we interview a candidate and what they tell us doesn't match with what they said in their resume.

As both our mothers used to teach us – the Truth never changes, and is easier to remember than a lie.

2. Don't puff. (No, we're not referring to President Clinton's assertion that he 'didn't inhale' when asked if he'd ever smoked marijuana!) Don't pretend you were more than you were in your previous jobs. We once hired a woman who interviewed well and looked great on her resume – she had all the right credentials, had done many of the things we needed done on the job, etc. We had very high hopes and expectations when we brought her in.

Because of her experience and background, we simply handed her large projects and said, "Go get 'im, Tiger." She failed miserably! She didn't have the first clue about how to do the job. Upon further investigation with her, she admitted she hadn't really led those large projects she cited on her resume – she helped out. She had a small part in them. Someone else had been the leader; she just carried out the instructions she was given. All of this became apparent when she was handed the baton and told to run with our projects.

The good news is that she got the job. The bad news is that she got fired from the job for incompetence. Don't let that happen to you.

3. No typos. Please understand you cannot afford to have typos in your resumes. Review your resume multiple times, reading slowly and critically. Ask a friend (not a spouse or parent) to review your resume – and ask them for any suggestions at all, even if they think they are minor.

4. No grammar difficulties. Sometimes as you craft your resume, you may add or delete items without changing the rest of the sentence, which in turn causes grammar difficulties. For example, here is an entry from a resume:

> Established national contracts with several recruiters, negotiating a lower rate than was normally offered.

But then the applicant decided to change the sentence a bit to:

> Established national contracts with several recruiters, negotiating lower rates than was normally offered.

Since they changed rate to rates, they should have changed the word was to were, since rates is plural:

> Established national contracts with several recruiters, negotiating lower rates than were normally offered.

5. Not tailored. By now you should realize the value and criticality of tailoring your resume for and to every job for which you apply. Thinking of doing otherwise (i.e. – submitting a generic resume to a job) should just give you the heebie-jeebies.

6. Too general. This item goes hand-in-hand with #6 – sometimes candidates try to be "all things to all people" and they'll submit a very general, broad resume. Instead, they come across as "no things to any people."

7. Too busy. As you craft your resume, be aware of the look and feel it has. Does it look cramped? Have you shrunk the margins at the top, bottom and sides to help you keep your resume to two pages? Does the reader get eye-whiplash looking from one bolded, underlined italicized and otherwise formatted element or your resume to another? Judicious formatting is good, just don't overload your readers.

8. Incorrect Contact information. While it doesn't happen often, we have on occasion reached out to a candidate and their contact information was incorrect – their e-mail address was mis-typed, or their phone number had been disconnected. Sometimes people will change their e-mail addresses because their spam filters have ceased to be effective…but they forget to change their e-mail address on their resume. Don't let that be you!

9. No achievement statements. You should be homed in on providing meaningful achievement statements on your resume, not just a list of tasks and responsibilities you performed on the job. Achievement statements tell your resume reviewers that you are more than a run-of-the-mill candidate.

10. Wrong Objective Statement. If you have an Objective statement, it's probably wrong anyway, since we prefer to see Summary statements. But beyond that, we have to smile as we read someone's Objective statement that tells us they want to work in the Healthcare industry…when we am not in the Healthcare industry. Again – do not let this be you.

11. Paragraphs vs. bullet points. Busy HR departments, recruiters and hiring managers don't have time to read lengthy paragraphs on resumes, looking for experiences that apply to the job they have open. It is best to bulletize your key points, rather than put them in paragraph form. Consider the difference between these two entries, identical except one is in paragraph form, the other is bulletized:

Coordinate the Public Affairs activities at 17 bases and stations throughout the Marine Forces Pacific Area of Operations. Responsible for the planning and execution of PA engagement for exercises and contingencies. Deployed to conduct PA support for Humanitarian Relief operations following a tsunami in Burma. Routinely coordinated MARFORPAC PA activities with State Department personnel at U.S. Embassies throughout the Asia / Pacific region and with our higher headquarters. Directly supported commander and senior staff in all facets of Public Affairs activities including: acting as spokesperson, preparing for and facilitating interviews, creating talking points, strategic messages and identifying opportunities for engagement.

- Coordinate the Public Affairs activities at 17 bases and stations throughout the Marine Forces Pacific Area of Operations. Responsible for the planning and execution of PA engagement for exercises and contingencies.
- Deployed to conduct PA support for Humanitarian Relief operations following a tsunami in Burma.
- Routinely coordinated MARFORPAC PA activities with State Department personnel at U.S. Embassies throughout the Asia / Pacific region and with our higher headquarters.
- Directly supported commander and senior staff in all facets of Public Affairs activities including: acting as spokesperson, preparing for and facilitating interviews, creating talking points, strategic messages and identifying opportunities for engagement.

We think they are easier and quicker to read as bullet points, rather than paragraphs.

12. Too many acronyms. This is a caution for military men and women in particular, but no industry is immune. Just because you know what an acronym means, and maybe even the hiring manager, the recruiter or HR professional may not. The first time you use an acronym, spell it out, followed by the acronym in parenthesis. Then you can use just the acronym later in your resume. For example: Certified Fraud Examiner (CFE). Make sure the resume screener understands the language you are speaking.

13. References available upon request. Please don't include this statement. We always assume references are available upon request. It merely takes up space, and doesn't add a thing to your resume. Use the space to tell us again what a great candidate you are by providing one more achievement statement that might catch our eye.

That doesn't mean you can't add your references as part of your resume. Generally, your references should be included on separate page. If that makes your resume three pages, that's okay – we don't really count the References page as part of the resume. If you are early in your career, it may be the second page of your resume, or even the last half / third or your second page. That is okay.

14. Personal information. Please don't put personal information on your resume, like your hobbies, spouse's and children's names, hobbies, sports teams, etc.

So – there you have it: a quick glance at things you need to pay attention to as you assemble your resume.

Common Resume Errors checklist

_____ Be honest on my resume – don't puff my experiences.

_____ Carefully proofread my resume multiple times.

_____ Tailor my resume to every job.

_____ Make sure my contact information is correct.

_____ Is my resume too acronymical, without spelling out what the acronym stands for at least once, the first time I use it?

_____ Put as many achievement statements in my resume as I can.

_____ Change my Objective statement to a Summary statement and make certain it matches the position for which I am applying.

In Closing

Let's pause now as you are nearing the end of this book and review some of the key points we made throughout these pages.

Are you ready to go get *That* Job, *The* Job? You know – the job you look forward to getting out of bed to go to. We have just delivered the most powerful job-seeking strategies we have seen. And by powerful we mean: proven successful and truly empowering. It is all about getting the job. Never, we mean *never* forget that!

Do you recall what we told you in Chapter 4 of this book?

> *Your only real goal and objective is to get "The Job." Never – and we mean NEVER – forget that. It is not about how many resumes you sent, or how many interviews you got (or didn't get), who you know or don't know. It is all about getting The Job. Period. But like all real goals there is a plan of milestones to meet. A successful business is more than an idea. It is a detailed, fluid plan built on experience and knowledge. That experience and knowledge teaches what must be firmly entrenched and what must be flexible. Please pay attention to these. It is very important to your successful job hunt.*

The milestones you *must* have are these:

    1. Professional-looking portrait for LinkedIn profile. Your profile will be 14% more likely to be looked at if you do.

    2. Know how to write an achievement statement tailored to;

    a. Each qualification on each job posting you apply for

    b. Demonstrate your results in a meaningful manner

3. Know how to build a LinkedIn profile, using achievement statements, based on six current job postings for which you are at least 80% qualified.

4. Get four to six recommendations relative to the six job postings referred to in #3 above from:

    a. Supervisors

    b. Peers

    c. Direct Reports

    d. Customers

    e. Vendors

    f. Competitors

5. Use the keywords and phrases from the job postings in all your written communications (online as well as paper).

6. Make at least 500 LinkedIn connections in your industry. Connect with company and professional recruiters, Human Resource professionals, managers of the teams you would be contributing to – these should be your primary focus. Everybody knows somebody. The more the merrier!

7. Follow and be followed on LinkedIn and Twitter by industry decision makers and companies. In your life, the decision makers are those individuals who can:

    a. Hire you

    b. Interview you

      c. Carry your profile and resume to those who can interview and hire you.

Connect with at least 500 recruiters, HR professionals and managers.

      8. Write a powerful resume tailored for each and every job for which you apply, addressing the pain points of that employer.

      9. You MUST, ABSOLUTELY MUST, demonstrate your results in a meaningful manner to the employer.

(A colleague of ours says that nine is a bad number. Apparently it is the number of death and hell in Mayan mythology. So if you are concerned about such things below are two more for you: eleven is a much better number. A prime number.)

      10. Build your network three layers deep. You know somebody (1st layer) who knows somebody (2nd layer) who knows somebody (3rd layer). LinkedIn names these layers, 1st, 2nd and 3rd connections.

      11. Facebook. Make it Puritan clean.

Next we will review some **flexible milestones**. Notice, these are fewer!

      1. LinkedIn endorsements. Get a bunch, but don't lose any brain cells over it. They are not worth the damage.

      2. Follow companies on Facebook. There are very valuable network connections to be made here and information to be found. But it is not a deal breaker.

      3. Twitter…. same as #2 Facebook. (That was easy.)

      4. Show all your language skills on LinkedIn.

      5. Show your Volunteer experience. This is very important, but not a deal breaker. It is more along the lines of demonstrating you understand and fit in the company culture.

6. Keep your political tone at a minimum or remove it altogether from your social media sites.

There you go. Half as many flexible milestones.

You might think we have forgotten about blogs, online portfolios and web pages. Nope, we did not. We don't consider them "milestones." Blogs, online portfolios and webpages are the true showcase of your industry expertise. Each blog posting must (oops, another 'must') be written to the level of an "A" level university paper. If you have a graduate degree, to a graduate level "A." If you have an MBA, you better write like it. Not to do so is to send a mixed message you do not want to send.

Online portfolios will bring the pop to your readers' experience with you before they even get the chance to shake your hand. Beautiful graphics, fun and interesting photographs of your work, you interacting with clients and shaking hands with industry leaders. All good! Remember, portfolios are not limited to artists, designers and architects. Engineers, oil field personnel, even scuba instructors can all gain from portfolios! Anyone who can tell a story with images.

Web pages are very useful for organizing loads of material, demonstrating efficiency and logic as well as creative problem solving. Just like online portfolios are not limited to artists, web pages are not limited to web masters.

Twitter is its own little animal. The primary purpose is to notify the interested world of your blog, online portfolio and / or web page. It is the oil that keeps the machine running. There are also good connections and intelligent information to be discovered and used on Twitter. (Remember the whole "homework" exercise we did?) Use G+ the same way.

Facebook contains a ready and very able networking group for you. And nearly anyone will be your friend there! People are good, and by merely asking for some help, you will get it. And when you land *The Job, That Job*, they – along with Lance and Dan – will celebrate with you.

Like Julius Caesar supposedly said, *"Veni, vidi, vici."* That is: "I came, I saw, I conquered." So go forth and conquer. After all, "Knowledge is power.

Power to change, power to influence, power to grow." Besides, you bought the book, so DO IT.

In Closing checklist

_____ Am I ready to get The Job – That Job?

_____ Tailor my resume to each job for which I apply.

_____ Quantify my accomplishments on my resume.

_____ Follow companies on Facebook.

_____ Follow companies and individuals on LinkedIn and Twitter.

_____ My Facebook must be Puritan clean.

_____ Blogs, online portfolios and webpages are the true showcase of my industry expertise.

_____ *Veni, vidi, vici!*

Index

ABOUT THE AUTHORS

Dan Quillen has been a professional in Human Resources for nearly twenty-five years. For a decade, he was the Director of Human Resources for one of the largest law firms in the western United States. Currently he is the Director of Internal Services (managing Human Resources, Purchasing, Risk and Fleet) for the City of Aurora, the third-largest city in Colorado.

For years, Dan has been an active mentor for those who were out of work, freely sharing his expertise in resume review and creation, interviewing and job searching. When not doing HR, Dan is a professional writer specializing in travel, technical and how-to subjects. He has written and published eighteen books on various topics. Dan makes his home in Centennial, Colorado.

Dr. Lance Farr has pioneered and directed a Social Media initiative with professionals to enhance candidate job searches while decreasing unemployment time to an average of 30 days. This is successfully accomplished by integrating Linked In, Twitter, Facebook and a blog in an intelligent and directed manner. This strategy has resulted in increased job seekers' search and reemployment success by dramatically increasing their relevance, visibility and exposure to targeted employers. For the past six years, Lance has worked closely with a multitude of job seekers, helping them integrate social media into their job searches to enable them to maximize the use of the tools available to them in their job search. A colleague of Lance's made this comment about him in his LinkedIn endorsement:

> *Lance is a powerful presenter and has a great teaching style. He is effective in presenting complex topics and taking advantage of social media to make his point. He has a great classroom personality. It is a pleasure to be in one of his classes.* – Tom Floodeen, LinkedIn endorsement for Dr. Lance Farr

If you'd like to contact the authors about anything in this book, their e-mail address is: **SocialMedia4DreamJob@gmail.com**. The authors welcome your comments and questions.

NOTES

Interested in delving deeper into the topics covered in this book? Dan Quillen has put his 25 years of HR hiring experience into *Get a Job! How I Found a Job When Jobs are Hard to Find – And So Can You.* All aspects of job searching are covered, including resumes, interviews, cover letters, networking, and much more!

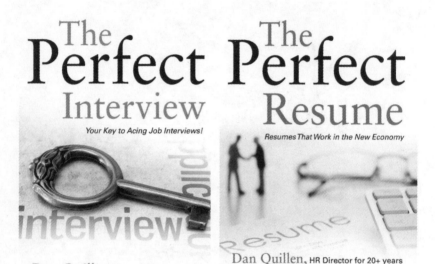